SELL
YOUR
BUSINESS

A PRACTICAL GUIDE
TO SUCCESSFULLY
SELLING YOUR BUSINESS

ANDREW ANDREYEV

Andreyev

First paperback edition published November 2022.

ISBN 978-0-6456097-0-7 (paperback)

ISBN 978-0-6456097-1-4 (ebook)

Published by Andreyev Press www.andreyev.com.au

Contents

1

Introduction

Building and running a business is challenging and often fun. It's no doubt one of the most rewarding things you've done. But the time has come for you to move on to a new chapter in life. It may be retirement, or it may simply be a change.

In this book we'll walk you through what's involved in successfully selling your business. From the first tentative step, all the way to the first sip of champagne.

Don't be fooled, selling your business is not going to be a simple task. There will be setbacks, frustrations and disappointments along the way. But we'll be there to offer you a clear roadmap to successfully navigate this unfamiliar landscape.

Meet Mal the truckie

In this book we're going to explore the ins and outs of the sale of Malcolm's transport business.

Case Study

Malcolm, or 'Mal' as he's known to his mates, is 56. He runs a transport business called Been There Logistics (**BTL**).

BTL has three main clients, and then many smaller clients.

Mal operates the business through a company (**BTL Pty Ltd**), which holds most of the plant, equipment, the brand, and any 'goodwill'.

In turn, BTL Pty Ltd is owned by the Been There Trust (the **Family Trust**).

The business started from a facility in Sydney, which is owned by the Family Trust. BTL also shares facility space in Newcastle and Melbourne.

Mal owns all the shares in another company, BTL Holdings Pty Ltd (**BTL Holdings**). BTL Holdings is the trustee of the Family Trust, has significant accumulated profits, and holds several prime movers recently purchased for the business.

Because Mal has been self-employed for most of his working life, he has very limited savings in superannuation.

Mal's father started the business back in **1980**. Mal and his brother John took the business over from their late father in **1997**. Mal bought John's interest in **2005**, thereby becoming the sole owner.

The business has a mix of in-house and contract drivers.

James is the manager of the business. He has worked for Mal for the past 8 years, having previously worked in the head office of a large national logistics company. He has a young family. James has a friend, Edward, who works in investment banking, and who is looking to invest some surplus money into a business. James also has some 'family money'.

Mal's objective is to step back from the business.

The legal structure for BTL is as follows:

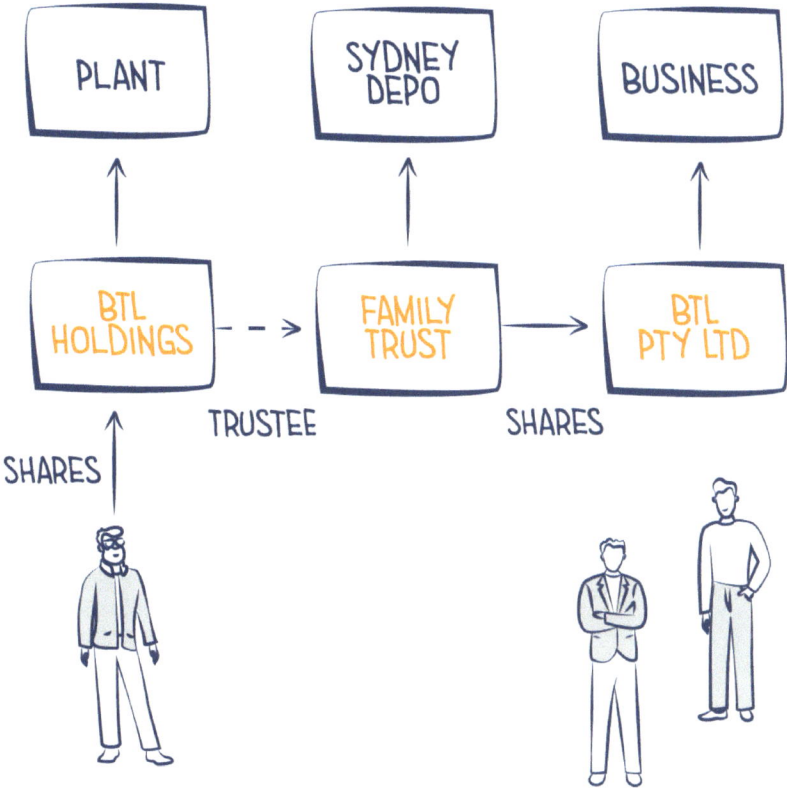

2

What's Your Strategy?

Do you have an exit strategy?

If you're like most businesspeople, you're working hard in your business to provide a nest egg for your retirement and to provide financial security and a legacy for your family.

However, statistically, most small and medium sized businesses are either **closed or given away**. Very few are sold for a meaningful amount of money.

Unfortunately, many businesspeople are forced into the sale process by **things they can't control** – by sickness, disability, a loss of key staff or a loss of key customers. Other businesses are left in the inexperienced hands of grieving family members through unexpected death.

You obviously want to avoid these scenarios.

The threshold issue for you to consider is whether you are in **control of your exit**? Have you put in place a plan for the short, medium and long term?

Ask yourself the following questions:

- ☑ Have you planned **when** you will exit your business? Do you have a date?

- ☑ Have you planned **how** you will exit your business? Do you have an exit strategy?

- ☑ At the end of the day, will you and your family reap the benefits of your hard work?

When should you be thinking about these issues?

As odd as it may sound, the best time to start thinking about selling your business is when you **first start setting it up**, (that's how successful 'serial entrepreneurs' do it). If you've already been in business for a while and haven't thought too much about getting out, don't worry, the second-best time to start planning your exit is **now**!

Do you own a business, or are you tied to a job?

For many business owners, the success or failure of their business depends on them turning up each day. If you are one of these business owners, you don't yet have anything of value to sell – your business is a 'job', not an investment.

Furthermore, it's probably the worst job you're likely to ever have. You probably haven't taken all your 'leave entitlements', you're probably underpaid for what you do, and you are carrying the ultimate financial and emotional responsibility for success or failure.

To avoid this common dilemma, you should seek to **make yourself redundant**, from day one (or as close to day one as possible). Yes, we are stating the obvious, and nothing that hasn't already been said by the likes of Michael Gerber[1] in the E-Myth book and many others. But that doesn't make it any less true.

People and processes should be established so that your **business runs without you being present**. This takes a lot of planning, system building and efficient execution. All of which should occur, or at the very least be contemplated, when you first set out on this journey.

Adopting this approach takes a lot of confidence – in yourself, your staff and your systems. But it's worth it.

Some helpful steps to kick this approach off include:

Invest heavily in systems

You need to move the management of your business out of your own head and into a standalone 'business system'. We've already noted that there are some excellent books and courses on how to do this.

The best way to make it happen is to hire an **experienced coach** and then invest heavily in terms of your time, your employee's time and your cash, and make it happen.

Develop a talented team

Selling to one or more key employees is usually a realistic exit option. However, even if you are not looking to sell to your employees, a third-party buyer will place a premium value on a **well-rounded and competent team**. In the high-tech sector, large businesses have paid premium value for small enterprises based solely on the talent of their team – a transaction that has come to be known as an 'acqui-hire' (acquisition-hiring).

Take on a professional manager

Finding a competent manager is a good start, but even more ideally you should build a **management team**, and then give them real autonomy and authority over your business. This goes together with developing your systems.

You may be able to find 'management talent' within your existing team, but often this is not the case. As your business has grown it is very likely to have hit a point where the original team just doesn't know how to take it any further. You're probably going to have to **look outside your existing team** to find the talent to set your business up for the exit.

The great thing about a management team is that they add real '**equity value**' to your business, but the team is unlikely to cost you too much in terms of 'equity'.[2] This means an overall **higher exit value** to you in the medium to longer term.

That said, professional management is likely to cost you more in terms of cash-flow and **reduced profitability** in the short term. This is the reason why most people end up with a business with nothing between themselves and lower-level employees – and hence with no real equity value.

Move family members out of your business

Unless you are intending to sell your business to your family, the sooner you move family members out of your business the better. The existence of family in your business will have a significantly negative impact on its value to a potential buyer. Whether you like it or not, a buyer will discount what they pay because you will not be able to convince them that your family will put the buyer's interests before yours (and their own).

As you work towards an exist you should be replacing family members with independent employees, executives and managers – so when you take your business to market, potential buyers can see that they are acquiring a **standalone enterprise** with few ties back to you.

Take on a business partner

Cultivating a management team is vastly preferable to taking on business partners. However, if you cannot build a management team, then taking on one or more partners is the next best step.

Preferably your partners will be at least half a generation younger than you and have skills that not only fill a current role in your business, but also provide an opportunity to take your business to the next level. For example, a younger partner may have a deep interest in marketing, technology, coding, media or exporting.

The key thing to look for in a business partner is someone genuinely willing and ultimately capably of running the business without you. If they do not have these attributes, then you are just diluting your equity value for no real benefit (other than perhaps someone to share a glass of red with at the end of a hard week).

Your 'Plan B'

The most valuable aspect of setting up your business to run without you is that it immediately creates '**competitive tension**' with your prospective buyers. You have, in effect, created a credible '**Plan B**' to being forced to sell or wind down your business. The importance of competitive tension, and how to develop and manage it, is discussed in more detail later.

Case Study

Mal has been partially successful in implementing his Plan B. Mal finally took the plunge and appointed *James* as the Manager when he had a health scare 5 years ago. James has turned out better than Mal expected. Initially, Mal was worried that James did not have enough 'real world experience' having only worked in an executive role.

James has been successful in implementing a new accounting and quoting system, and James has also put in place a solid 'reporting' framework to keep Mal informed about the key business metrics.

But Mal still finds himself drawn back into certain aspects of the business, namely dealing with his three key clients, making the decisions about buying large pieces of equipment and mediating disputes between some of his long-term staff.

So far Mal has not been able to put in place a way for key, high-level decisions to be made without him. He thinks this is because people like James still don't have any 'skin in the game'. James also lacks deep experience in the trucking game, having come more from an accounting and finance background.

To complete his implementation of an effective Plan B, Mal either needs to up-skill James to be able to make these bigger decisions or look for other executives who can fill the gaps. He may wish to find an executive with deep logistics experience. He may also wish to establish an 'advisory board' consisting of senior people who can support and mentor James. Mal also needs to deliberately stand back from his key client relationships and make space for others to build rapport.

Some relevant statistics

There are not a lot of statistics on private business sales (and other exits) in Australia. The Australian Bureau of Statics compiles high-level statics on the formation and dissolution of business entities, but there is little direct data how many business owners achieve a successful exit.

A Commonwealth Bank of Australia *Local Business Owner Report found that:*[3]

- ☑ Only 47% of small business owners have an actual exit strategy.
- ☑ 22% of those who do have an exit plan simply intend to close the doors and walk away.
- ☑ 60% of small business owners are still actively reinvesting profits back into their businesses, and half are working more than 50 hours a week, even though statistics suggest those businesses will eventually be closed.
- ☑ 25% of business owners aged over 60 are planning to close their businesses at retirement.

The ABN data indicates that around 60% of SME businesses in Australia are owned by people over the age of 45. Around 20% are owned by people over 60.[4]

Finally, the worst statistic of them all, it is estimated that out of all the 'exits' each year, less than 2% of private business owners get to 'voluntarily' exit their business by sale or takeover. The same study concludes that a **lack of planning** is a major contributor to this outcome.

Setting a date with destiny

Irrespective of how far developed you are with your Plan B, you need to set a firm date for having a solid Plan B in place, and then another date for exiting your business. If on reflection your business still represents more of a 'job' than an 'investment', then the timeframe to sell is likely to be longer than if you already have a solid Plan B in place.

Take the time now to **write down the date** on which you plan to sign the documents to sell your business. Let us now work backwards from there.

Your growth strategy

The saying goes that your business is either growing or dying. If you ultimately want to get excellent value for your business, then you need to have a **clear 'growth strategy'**. (You obviously don't want to adopt the 'death strategy' by default!)

You may be thinking – why do I need a growth strategy right at the time I'm thinking about selling? You are not just selling the current 'realised' value of your business. You also want to get some value for all the **future opportunities** you have laid the groundwork for. This puts the sizzle into the sale, and into the price you receive.

Put yourself in the shoes of the buyer – they want to feel there is some **genuine 'upside' in the business**, and you want them focusing on potential gains, not potential risks and failure.

You can pursue growth in several ways. You can:

- Spend time and money on **marketing** - to acquire new customers in an existing market or in new markets;

- Spend time and money on **training** and **R&D** – to expand your product range and service offerings; or

- **Purchase** existing customers, existing products and existing capabilities from other businesses.

The first two options (the 'do-it-yourself' options) are commonly referred to as *organic growth,* and the last option is *growth by acquisition*.

Most businesses actively engage in organic growth through marketing and training. Some also pursue organic growth through product or service innovation (i.e. R&D). However, very few small to medium sized businesses actively explore growth opportunities through acquisition, despite the apparent flood of business owners looking for an exit strategy.

This can be contrasted with most large businesses, which actively pursue growth through acquisition (as well as organically). Unlike most smaller businesses, large businesses recognise that sensible growth through acquisition can reduce the risk of failed innovation and offer skills, experience and customers they may not otherwise attain through organic growth.

If you want to end up with a valuable business, and differentiate yourself from the crowd, then you should be pro-active about **growth by acquisition**.

You may be surprised to learn that simply approaching others in your industry, proposing an exit strategy, and doing some of the 'heavy lifting' for them, can result in an opportunity for you to purchase a complimentary business at a bargain price.

You should also actively involve your advisers in **finding acquisitions for you**. Advisers, like your banker, lawyer, accountant, financial planner and insurance broker are uniquely placed to identify opportunities that may not otherwise be readily apparent to you.

'Business succession' is a vitally important area, but many advisers unfortunately fail to see that the flip side of business succession is a large and important opportunity to facilitate growth by acquisitions. If you are a business adviser reading this book, then the time is ripe for you to focus as much on **finding acquisitions for your clients**, as it is for helping them with business succession. They're just different sides of the same coin.

Case Study

For some time, Mal has been working closely with two other smaller transport operators.

One business is owned by someone Mal's own age, Alex. Alex is in poor health and his business has become more and more reliant on Mal's assistance.

The other business is operated by Ken, who is much younger than Mal. Ken started out as a driver like Mal and has brought some unique loading/unloading concepts to the market and cut costs. But Ken is struggling to get scale and is often strapped for cash.

These two businesses represent a great opportunity for Mal to acquire clients, revenue, assets and technology.

In addition, combining with Ken's business represents an opportunity to acquire Ken's unique skills that will compliment James' weaknesses in operations. Ken may also be prepared to take some 'equity' in Mal's business as part of a 'merger' rather than a straight-out acquisition.

Once again, Mal is excited about the opportunity to grow BTL, but this excitement is soon tempered by the pile of things he already needs to get through on his desk...!

3

What's it Like to Sell a Business?

It's never simple

You will soon discover that buying or selling a business is a major event. Transactions are seldom simple, largely because you are selling a 'living organism' that won't stand still just because you think it's time to move on.

If you are a prospective buyer, purchasing the wrong business, overpaying for the right business, or simply failing to adequately structure or document the transaction doesn't just cost you additional interest (on borrowed money used to finance the purchase) but unnecessarily wastes your hard-earned equity.

Conversely, as a prospective seller, failure to adequately structure or document the transaction may result in a big chunk of the cash you receive on settlement being quickly taken away from you by the Tax Man, creditors and even the buyer.

Good advisers (on both sides) must strive for a 'fair deal,' where:

- You, as either seller or buyer, can follow a clear process;

- The parties on both sides are well informed; and

- The risks and benefits of doing the deal are clearly allocated between the parties as follows:

  - First, according to their **ability to manage the risk** (because this will minimise the cost-impact of the risks); and

  - Second, according to their **bargaining positions**.

Avoid harmful distractions

Given these transactions are complex, involve multiple parties (owners and buyers and their respective advisers, employees, customers, suppliers, banks etc.) and are often completed in relatively short timeframes, there will be a tendency for you to quickly become tired and **emotional**. 'Deal fatigue' or 'deal fixation' can soon set in. You are also likely to have to make decisions under **pressure**. Once a deal 'is on' you might even find yourself **feeling pressured or 'obliged' to commit** to a particular outcome, notwithstanding it's not ideal.

Simply having an awareness of the possibility (probability) that you may experience these emotions and circumstances is a key first step to helping you manage them. Equally important is your discipline around avoiding harmful distractions.

If you are a prospective seller, it's important that you continue to commit the necessary resources (in time, capital and people) to **preserving the value of the business you are selling**. If the sale process drags on too long, there is a greater risk that the value of the business may be (inadvertently) impaired by the process of trying to sell.

If you are a prospective buyer, it's important that you remain focused on the task at hand – **purchasing the right business for the right price** – rather than allowing human emotion or ego to influence your decision making.

Your **Deal Team** should consist of a mix of internal resources and external advisers. Internally, this will usually involve the time of the CEO, the COO and the CFO. It is also a good idea to identify one or two 'lackies' that can help assemble information and responses to the buyer's team. Externally, at a minimum you will need to involve your lawyer, accountant, banker and insurance broker.

Case Study

To minimise the distractions to his day-to-day business operations, Mal has taken advice to 'quarantine' the sale process to a limited number of his staff – *the 'Deal Team'*.

The rest of his business will be insulated from the sale process. They will be informed of what is going on, so they don't feel left out, but they will be expected to pick up some slack from the Deal Team members and ensure that the business continues to service its clients and sustain and grow the core business.

Mal's deal team initially consist of James, Mel (Mal's PA), Mal's accountant Doreen and his lawyer Louise.

Seek the right advice

Using **good judgment** is one of the most critical, but often ignored, factors influencing the outcome of your negotiation to buy or sell a business.

It is good judgment that tells you when to stand firm on an issue of critical importance, and when to stand down or show flexibility on an issue of less importance.

In the heat of the moment, it is often difficult to exercise sound, objective judgment, which is why it's important to be surrounded by a good team of experienced advisers who can provide objective guidance. You want committed and responsive advisers, but you also need advisers who are not emotionally invested in the transaction like you will be.

You should plan, upfront, to seek the assistance of good advisers, and to be prepared to listen to their advice. At the end of this book we offer some further practical guidance on how to select and appoint your advisers.

Case Study

Mal has had a long-standing relationship with his accountant, Doreen. He has dealt with his lawyer, Louise, on several occasions over the past few years, when purchasing property and entering a major contract, but he does not know her particularly well.

Mal calls a meeting with his accountant and lawyer to make sure they are happy to be on the Deal Team. He also asks them to recommend anyone else who should be involved in the deal.

Louise suggests that at some stage it may be prudent to get a corporate finance adviser involved, someone who has the dedicated resources to help with running the deal and helping with valuation and sale price issues. Doreen pushes back on this, as she feels this encroaches on her space as Mal's accountant. But after some discussion, Doreen acknowledges that she really doesn't have the capacity to do everything associated with the deal.

The team identifies that they will need to let Mal's bankers know what is planned. They will also need to speak with a few external 'subject matter experts', like Mal's insurance broker and property manager.

James proposes to involve his investment banking friend, Edward.

During the next few Deal Team meetings James and Edward soon get excited about the prospect of taking over or merging with Alex and Ken's businesses. Mal is more focused on his exit, but is encouraged to see the strong buy-in from James, as well as Edward's level of excitement about the opportunities.

4

Understand Your Motivations

Articulate your reasons for selling

If you are contemplating a particular transaction, it is critical that you clearly answer the following question before you embark on the process:

*What is motivating you to consider selling
or buying this business, at this time?*

You should **write your answer down**, so that when things get tough, in the heat of the moment, you can readily refer to it for guidance, and to help you stay on track.

Some common reasons that may be motivating you to consider selling your business include:

- Retirement;

- Plans to travel;

- 'Cashing-out';

- Simplifying life;

- Starting a new business; or

- Embarking on a new challenge.

Some common reasons why someone might want to buy a business include:

- Transitioning from paid employment, i.e. 'buying a job';

- Extending a product range;

- Removing competition;

- Vertically integrating their business with suppliers and customers; or

- Seeking economies of scale.

It is not enough to simply identify the reason or motivation for a proposed sale or purchase. Just as important is an analysis of whether the proposed transaction will ultimately deliver your desired outcome. If you are interested in selling your business to fund your retirement, the question becomes: 'Will the sale achieve a price sufficient to fund my retirement?' If it won't, then you will need to consider other options.

Do you just need a break?

You might be like many business owners who frequently indicate a desire to sell a business, when in fact all you really want (or need) is to just **take a break**. Such exhausted business owners often start the sale process and then pull back when reality takes hold. Therefore, we suggest you perform the following 'Reality Check' before embarking on the sale process.

Undertake a 'Reality Check'

Before you embark on the sale of your business, you should answer 'Yes!' to each of the following questions:

- ☑ Have you recently taken a **long break** from your business?

- ☑ Do you want to be **relieved of the responsibility** of managing your business?

- ☑ Do you have plans or **other things to do** after your business is off your hands?

- ☑ Have you **considered other options** to selling, such as becoming a silent partner, or hiring outside management?

- ☑ Is it the **right time** to sell your business? Consider this question in terms of both the market and your professional and personal goals.

- ☑ Do you believe you will achieve a higher price by selling your business now, as opposed to waiting a few months or even a few years?

- ☑ Will selling your business ultimately benefit you financially? What analysis have you done to prove this?

- ☑ Do you feel your **life will be made easier** if you sell your business?

- ☑ Will you be **free to earn a living** after the sale, or might some of the proposed sale terms prohibit you from engaging in certain activities?

- ☑ Is your **family** on board with the sale of your business?

- ☑ Are you **emotionally** ready to sell your business?

Case Study

Mal is only 56. He's still young and will need to find other things to keep him busy after his sale of BTL.

He has been working in the family business since he was a teenager. He has 'carried the can' for the entire business since his brother left in 2005. He has not had a proper holiday in over 4 years.

Mal has considered the option of passing the business over entirely to 'professional management', but has found it hard to let go in the past when others have tried to step-up into a more senior role.

We ask Mal to perform the 'Realty Check', and while his responses suggest he may be making his decision to sell because he is physically and emotionally exhausted, he is adamant that he wants to pursue the sale of BTL.

If this is the case, then it is worth moving forward, at least through the preparatory stages, where Mal will get a better idea of what he will end up with if a deal is ultimately done.

Mal is also coming around to the idea that he may retain some level of ownership in the business, at least in the medium term, particularly if a deal can be done with Alex and Ken to first expand the business to the 'next level'.

5

Before You Get Started

If you are a business owner and you decide to sell your business, you should **not** immediately start calling prospective buyers, as many business owners make the mistake of doing. It is unrealistic to launch straight into a formal sales process and expect to achieve an ideal outcome, being the maximum sale price through a cost-and-time efficient process.

We often see people contact someone they think 'may be interested' in their business, only to then find themselves in a 'sale process' being led by the potential buyer. The number one thing missing from these negotiations, which is critical to a successful outcome for the seller, is **competitive tension**.

As a prospective seller, you need to take the following preliminary steps before commencing the formal sales process, each of which will be considered in turn:

Do a **Business Review**	'Take stock' of what you are selling.
Get a rough **Business Valuation**	Get a real sense of what your business may be worth.
Work out what to sell and what to keep	Decide **what assets you wish to sell** and **what assets you wish to keep.**
Get 'sale ready'	**Get your business into shape** in anticipation of the sale.
Decide on the best **transaction structure**, i.e. between an 'Asset Sale' and an 'Entity Sale'	Work out whether you will get the best outcome from selling the assets of the business, or the business entity itself.
Do any necessary **'pre-sale restructuring'**	Implement any necessary pre-sale restructuring to get the business ready for sale and to maximise the sales price and minimise taxes.
Work out the **best way to get paid**	Give thought to how you would like to be paid, including if you are going to offer any 'vendor finance' to the buyer.

It is important to appreciate that pre-sale considerations are as important as the actual sales process itself. Proper planning facilitates proper execution.

What are you selling?

The first thing to do is clearly **identify what you have available to sell**. You do this by undertaking a review of your business assets and operations.

This process should include:

☑ Preparing **interim financial statements**, to provide a 'snap-shot' of the current financial state of your business.

☑ Updating the **schedule of plant and equipment**.

☑ Identifying **key customers** and **key suppliers**.

☑ Identifying **key employees**.

☑ Updating your **Business Plan** and **Marketing Plan** (yes, you have these... don't you?) These days many people prepare a 'Pitch Deck', rather than a Business Plan, but ultimately these contain similar information.

You can use some of this material later in the preparation of the **Information Memorandum**, so your time and effort will be well spent here, as it serves a dual purpose. Accountants, lawyers and other external business advisors can readily assist you in the business review process.

Case Study

Mal makes the following relevant information available to us:

The primary assets used in the business include:

Plant and equipment, including the truck fleet;

The Sydney facility (owned through Mal's Family Trust); and

Business 'goodwill' (associated with the client contracts and reputation).

The business has three key clients, representing about 30% of the turnover. The balance of turnover is spread over many small accounts.

The business has three key staff, including James, who is the manager.

Key financial data includes:

Annual turnover	$22.5 million
Annual profit	$2.8 million
Net book value of assets	$4.5 million
Council valuation of Sydney facility	$3.5 million

What is your business worth?

The process of selling your business starts with a solid understanding of the value you are likely to realise.

When each of the components of your business have been clearly identified, **you can form an <u>initial view</u> of the value of your business** 'as a whole', or each separately identifiable component of your business.

Interestingly, most business owners (and prospective buyers) tend to avoid directly confronting the issue of true value. Both buyers and sellers frequently take very subjective views of business value, **failing to perform enough financial (and other) analysis** to form a truly objective, and thus realistic, view of value.

Business owners will often express a (subjective) view on the value of their business, which (unsurprisingly) directly correlates to the amount of money they feel they need to fund their post-sale plans (such as retirement). Obviously, the amount of money required to fund post-sale plans is completely irrelevant to the true value of a business, determined objectively using financial (and other) analysis.

A poor understanding of the true value of your business upfront can cause the sale process to stall later. **Your expectations of value need to be managed at the very early stages of the process**.

Case Study

In initial conversations with Mal, he says he thinks his business is worth around $10 million.

When asked how he arrived at this number he says that it just 'feels about right'. When pushed, he says he thinks he could live comfortably on this amount. He admits that he really does not have a strong analytical basis for choosing this value.

Why is value important?

If you as a business owner don't know what your business may be objectively worth, you cannot make informed decisions about:

- Whether to sell your business;
- When to sell your business;
- How much of your business to sell;
- Who is likely to be able to purchase your business; and
- What you can do now to significantly increase the sale value later.

You need to clearly understand the **key drivers** of the value of your business. Failing this, you will not have the information necessary to preserve, increase or maximise business value in the event of a sale.

Naturally, if you are a prospective buyer, you will instead focus on the **risks** of taking over a business. A seller should be ready, willing and able to address (and neutralise) the risks you identify, as well as introduce you to **untapped opportunities** for future growth in business value.

The importance of listening to the market

You need to get in touch with the 'real market' for your business, and importantly, **listen to what the market is saying to you about your business' true value**. Your business will not be worth more just because you refuse to listen to factors that may impact it adversely (quite the contrary).

What to do if the market won't pay enough

If you find that the market will not put a value on your business that is sufficient to fund your post-sale plans (or otherwise), then the cold, hard, truth may be that you really aren't able to sell the business.

You are then left with three choices:

- Continue working more efficiently and effectively *in your business* to create incremental value (by increasing net operating income for example);

- Work harder *on your business* to increase its overall sale value; or

- *Adjust downward your post-sale lifestyle expectations*.

Be prepared for smaller investment returns

Another reality you must be prepared for is that you are very unlikely to achieve the same level of return investing the proceeds from the sale of your business, as you would have achieved had you continued to operate your business.

This is simply a function of the **risk-reward principle**. As a business owner, if you have taken 'equity' off the table (via a sale), placed that equity in a 'safer' investment, and you are no longer working 70+ hours per week, you can't (reasonably) expect to earn the same economic returns.

Case Study

If we assume Mal gets the $10 million he is hoping for from the sale of BTL, he still might not have enough money to fund his plans.

If he invests the proceeds at say 5% (which is still a good return in the current market), he will earn an annual income of $500,000, ignoring inflation. While this is a material sum of money, it is also a sizable discount to the $2.8 million annual pre-tax profit he is currently making from the business!

Perhaps if asked again, Mal might reconsider his view that he could live comfortably on the proceeds from the sale.

In short, as a business owner, you need to remain calm and detached, listen to the market, and rely on objective measures of the value of your business.

Why value is important to the buyer

There is little point in you looking to buy a business that you ultimately can't afford.

As a buyer, you also need a thorough understanding of the factors that determine a business' value, to reasonably assess what to pay. You should strive to realistically assess the **opportunities** and **risks** associated with the business – to determine whether you have the **skills** and **experience** to exploit those opportunities and manage the risks.

From our observations, inexperienced buyers are generally too risk-averse and often unrealistically expect to purchase a business at a below-bargain price. An experienced and informed buyer, on the other hand, is prepared to **pay a premium for a quality business**. Generally, you can almost never overpay for a great asset.

'Normalising' your financial information

Before applying any of the common approaches to determine the likely value of your business, the financial information being relied on needs to be 'normalised'. This means adjusting your accounting figures to reflect the **arm's length principle** and the **comparable principle**.

The 'arm's length' principle

Most privately held businesses are operated to fulfil a mix of 'business' and 'personal' objectives. This can result in an **overstatement** or **understatement** of both income and expenses – as compared with a business that enters every transaction with an unrelated third party or on arm's length terms, (e.g. a publicly listed company).

The real value of a business is determined with reference to what the income and expenses *would be* under the **arm's length principle**. Therefore, adjustments need to be made to the financial accounts to 'normalise' the related party transactions to comparable arm's length market rates.

Case Study

Mal does not draw a wage from his business. To do so would give rise to unnecessary workers' compensation levies and payroll taxes. Instead, Mal is content to earn higher profits on his equity in the business. These profits flow through the Family Trust and are then shared among the family.

On the other hand, BTL Pty Ltd pays 'top of the market' rent for use of the Sydney depot, as this moves profits out of the business entity and into the Family Trust. Although the rent is still within 'market parameters', it is less likely that a third party will readily agree to this 'premium' level of rent.

Mal's historical financial figures will need to be adjusted for both market realities, i.e. profit will be adjusted down by the market value of Mal's wage, and profit will be adjusted up to correct for a more acceptable market rent on the Sydney depot.

Closer examination may reveal other adjustments that are required to bring the accounts in-line with a true open market position.

The 'comparable' principle

In addition to adjustments to reflect the arm's length principle, the accounts also need to be adjusted for **one-off** or **abnormal** transactions.

Real business value is determined according to what can be expected to occur in the future, and some things that have occurred in the past are not likely to happen again. This can result in both positive and negative adjustments.

Case Study

Over the past 2 years Mal has been locked in a bitter dispute with a sub-contractor who failed to properly insure his rig and caused a significant loss. This resulted in legal fees of around $45,000, as well as a once-off settlement payment of a further $20,000.

As this dispute cannot be expected to occur again in the usual course of business, the expenses in these 2 years can be adjusted down, resulting in a higher normalised profit.

These adjustments are generally characterised as:

- Discretionary adjustments;
- Non-recurring adjustments;
- Non-operating adjustments; and
- Comparability adjustments.

Note:

A simple net asset calculation is typically based on the amounts reflected in the Balance Sheet, which is prepared using historical data. To obtain a better understanding of the true net 'value' of the business' assets, they are often adjusted to reflect current market values.

It is also necessary to determine whether adjustments are required for 'surplus' or 'non-operational' assets, which are assets that are not required or necessary for the continued conduct of the business.

Getting access to information

Getting access to the necessary market information to determine the value of your business can be time-consuming and expensive.

Accountants, financiers, bankers and business brokers are likely to have access to **industry databases** that can provide you with information on 'rates of return' and 'comparable industry multiples'. Your accountant can be particularly helpful to you in the process of adjusting and normalising your financial data.

Be aware that this industry information changes over time, in line with the state of the economy and changes in the industry you are in.

Other important sources of data available to you include:

- Industry research papers;

- Industry associations;

- Business-for-sale listings in industry magazines, newspapers and websites;

- Stock market analyses; and

- ASIC databases.

It is often difficult to select from, and then apply, appropriate industry data to arrive at a realistic value for your business, given that all businesses have unique attributes. This is when the process of valuation becomes more of an 'art', rather than a science – and where the true value of **perception**, **competitive tension** and the **ability to negotiate** come into play.

When to determine value

As a business owner, you should remain **periodically informed** on the likely value of your business. At the very least, you should assess the value of your business at the end of each financial year – as this will facilitate both short-term and long-term decision-making about your business operations.

Limiting this review to a 'P&L' or 'profitability analysis' ignores the **capital value** that you may be building within your business over time. Focusing only on your P&L will inevitably lead you to think short-term, and to underinvest in brand development, R&D, IP, systems and professional management.

Preparing a **valuation model** that is appropriate for your business should be a relatively straightforward process for your accountant or corporate adviser, and it should be a model that can be easily and periodically updated with the most current data.

Common approaches to determining value

The three most common approaches to determining a business' value are the **Income Approaches**, the **Market Approaches** and the **Asset Approaches**. It is good practice to apply as many of these approaches as possible to your business to get a broad perspective on its likely real value.

Income approaches to valuation

These approaches value the **expected future cash flows** or future 'earnings' from your business. Two examples of this approach include:

- Future Maintainable Earnings (FME); and

- Discounted Cash Flow (DCF).

Future Maintainable Earnings (FME)

The capitalisation of Future Maintainable Earnings method is one of the most common methods for valuing an existing small business, as it usually aligns reasonably well with the expectations of prospective buyers. It is a derivation or simplification of the **Discounted Cash Flow** method, discussed next.

This method involves multiplying an estimate of 'future maintainable earnings' (**FME**) by a 'capitalisation **multiple**' (**Cap Rate**):

FME x Cap Rate (multiple) = Business Value

If the Cap Rate is expressed as a **percentage** rather than a multiple, then the formula is:

$$FME / (Cap\ Rate\ (\%)) = Business\ Value$$

The future maintainable earnings are usually estimated with reference to the historical and forecast results of the business, adjusted for key industry risks, future growth prospects and the general economic outlook.

Settling on an appropriate 'Cap Rate' involves assessing the buyer's **required rate of return**, the **inherent risks** of the business, future **growth prospects** and the returns available on **alternative investments** (such as the 'risk-free' rate). The Cap Rate tries to synthesis all these elements of value into a single figure.

The higher the perceived risks for the business, the higher the required rate of return for the buyer, and the lower the Cap Rate multiple. This is the classic risk-return trade-off. As investments go, businesses are generally considered riskier than government bonds, property and listed shares, and therefore a Cap Rate of over *4 times* is quite rare, with *3 times* or less being quite common (although this has risen in recent times in line with the long-term falling trend in the risk-free rate of return). A Cap Rate of *4 times* is equivalent to a 25% annual return on investment.

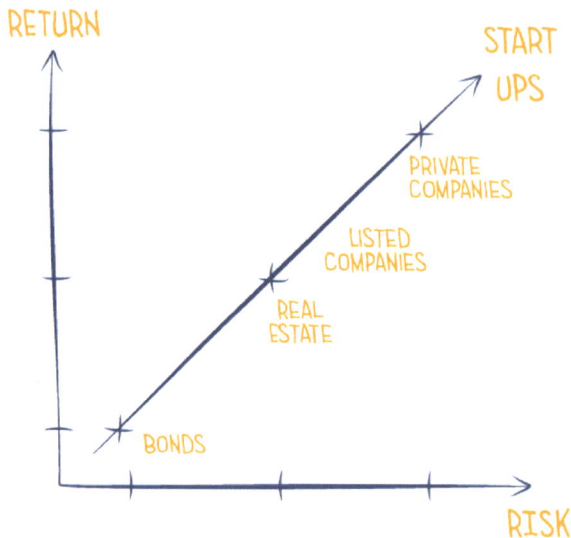

The actual Cap Rate for a business will be influenced by several factors, including the specific risks associated with the business and will generally range from as high as *8 times* (12.5% p.a., being a relatively low return), to as low as *1 times* (100% p.a. or equivalent to getting your money back each year) for private enterprises.

Note that to obtain a true value of your business, it may be necessary to adjust the raw business value for any **net 'surplus' or 'non-operational' items**, being those items that are not essential to the production of the future maintainable income.

Case Study

When valuing Mal's business we need to adjust his profits for the fact he has been underpaid as the manager, and that his wife has not been paid at all for her work in marketing.

We also need to remove the interest paid by the business on its bank loan, as we are basing the valuation on 'earnings before interest and tax' – EBIT. We do this because the way a business funds its assets and operations should not impact the valuation, i.e. we base the valuation on 'comparable un-geared businesses'. If we do not exclude the interest payments, then the underlying value of the business can be manipulated simply by increasing or decreasing the extent to which it is funded by debt.

Applying these adjustments to Mal's cash flow:

Future Maintainable Earnings

	20XX	20X1	20X2	Average
Revenue	22,450,000	20,750,000	24,400,000	22,533,333
Operating costs	(15,490,500)	(14,940,000)	(15,860,000)	(15,430,167)
Gross profit	6,959,500	5,810,000	8,540,000	7,103,167
Other expenses	(4,265,500)	(4,150,000)	(4,392,000)	(4,269,167)
Net profit	2,694,000	1,660,000	4,148,000	2,834,000

Adjustments

Wage for marketing support (currently done by Mal's wife for no wage)	(110,000)
Wage for Manager (market-level wage to replace Mal)	(180,000)
Owners' wages and benefits (adding back the value of 'benefits' Mal receives)	90,000
Interest (Adding back interest expensed within the business)	71,500
Market rent adjustment (Adding back 'top rate' rent)	40,000
Adjustment for once-off legal fees and settlement sum	65,000
Total adjusted profit	2,810,500

Cap Rate 35%

Value	**$8,030,000**

The Discounted Cash Flow method is another income approach and is used to value **new or immature businesses** (i.e. 'start-ups'), or business in which future income and/or expenditures are expected to vary widely from historical performance.

This method takes an estimate of *future* cash flows and then applies a 'discount rate' to arrive back at the 'present value' of those cash flows. The present value then being the current 'market value' of the business. The required discount rate increases with the risk-free rate, the level of risk inherent in the business, the industry in which the business operates and the estimated time taken for the business to reach maintainable earnings.

Applying this valuation method to Mal's business:

Discounted Cash-flow

Discount rate	30%
20X1	$2,700,000
20X2	$2,700,000
20X3	$2,750,000
20X4	$2,750,000
20X5	$2,800,000
20X6	$2,800,000
Present value	**$7,223,329**

It is commonly recognised that the Discounted Cash Flow method is the most 'academically pure' method of valuation. This is because it does not rely on *historical* performance, which may not represent likely *future* performance.

The difficulty is that this method requires a robust assessment of future net cash flows (investments, revenues, expenses and proceeds), which can be very hard (often impossible) to predict. Furthermore, the discount rate once again represents a synthesis of the various factors that are likely to influence the success (or failure) of the enterprise – which is necessarily subjective.

There is a clear trade-off between relying on historical earnings that may not be repeated (i.e. the FME method) and projecting likely future revenues which may be highly subjective (i.e. DCF method). Both methods then apply a highly subjective multiple or discount factor.

As a practical matter, if you have been making considerable investments in your business which have not yet born fruit, then you may wish to adopt the DCF method and include the *projected* (and justifiable) increase in future revenues, rather than the FME method.

Market approaches to valuation

The market approaches look to the value of other 'comparable' businesses that have been sold on the open market, and then apply a 'proxy' of that market value to the business being sold.

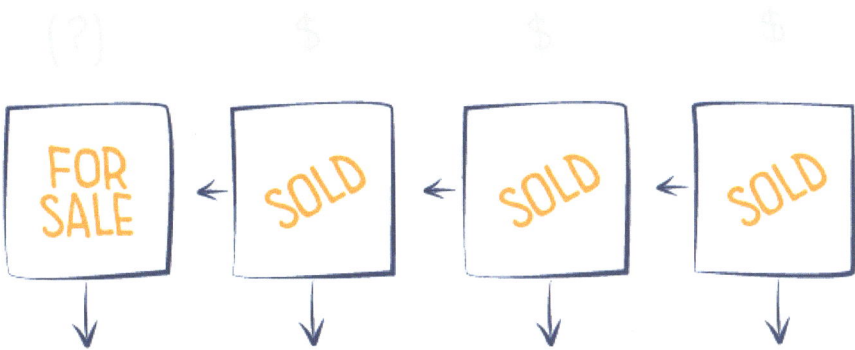

Earnings Multiple

The Earnings Multiple method determines the value of a business by observing the prices achieved for similar enterprises ('comparables') that have recently sold on the open market.

Under this method you take an average of historical earnings, typically before interest and tax (i.e. EBIT) and multiple it by a selected '**market multiple**'. For example, if you value a business on a multiple of '3', and it has historical EBIT of $500,000 p.a., then the business would have a value of $1,500,000.

The 'multiple' you choose is **market driven** and depends on the industry and the growth potential of the business you are valuing. A service-based business might demand a multiple as low as *1 x EBIT*, while an established business with sustainable profits in another industry might demand a multiple as high as *8 x EBIT*.

This method **relies very heavily on <u>recent sales</u>** of comparable businesses. The valuer must closely analyse (and compare) the characteristics of the businesses to determine 'comparability' and the multiple to be applied.

The Earnings Multiple method is quite widely adopted, especially for back-of-the-envelope or rule-of-thumb valuations. The downfall of this method is that it relies heavily on **market-based information**, and due to the confidential nature of private business sales, this information is often difficult to obtain.

In practical terms, the Earnings Multiple method and the Future Maintainable Earnings method are very similar. They both rely on applying a 'multiple' (or discount) to a projected earnings stream. The theoretical distinction is that the Earnings Method relies on comparable sales to set the multiple. Whereas in practical terms, so does the FME method!

Applying this valuation method to Mal's business:

Market Multiple

	20XX	20X1	20X2	Average
Revenue	22,450,000	20,750,000	24,400,000	22,533,333
Operating costs	(15,490,500)	(14,940,000)	(15,860,000)	(15,430,167)
Gross profit	6,959,500	5,810,000	8,540,000	7,103,167
Other expenses	(4,265,500)	(4,150,000)	(4,392,000)	(4,269,167)
Net profit	2,694,000	1,660,000	4,148,000	2,834,000

Adjustments

Wage for marketing support (currently done by Mal's wife for no wage)	(110,000)
Wage for Manager (market-level wage to replace Mal)	(180,000)
Owners' wages and benefits (adding back the value of 'benefits' Mal receives)	90,000
Interest (Adding back interest expensed within the business)	71,500
Market rent adjustment (Adding back 'top rate' rent)	40,000
Adjustment for once-off legal fees and settlement sum	65,000
Total adjusted profit	2,810,500
Value Market multiple 3	$8,431,500

Earnings multiples are only one market approach. Other market approaches include methods based on:

- Number of registered users (based on user/customer acquisition cost); and

- Gross revenue - as opposed to net profits - for professional services firms (e.g. accounting practices and financial planning firms often sell for a multiple of recurring revenue).

These multiple-based methods may be used when a business is still in a pre-revenue or pre-profit stage, and more robust valuation methods are otherwise difficult to apply. They are also applied in scenarios where there is a vibrant market for 'incremental revenue' among established industry participants looking for easy growth.

Asset approaches

Asset-based approaches look to the current market value of the assets (and liabilities) of the business on the assumption that the business is closed down, and the assets are sold off, (i.e. without the 'going concern' assumption).

Net Assets

The Net Asset value of a business is the difference between the realisable value of its 'assets' and its 'liabilities'. This method is essentially a proxy for the value of a business if it was closed and the parts sold off, or if the business had to be **built from scratch**.

This method ignores the value associated with the ability of *in situ* assets to *generate future income*, and therefore does not consider the value of any 'goodwill'. It also ignores the value of prior expenditure that has been 'expensed' for accounting purposes and therefore does not show up in the books.

However, it might be appropriate to apply this method if a business does not have any goodwill or has negative goodwill. The underlying assumption is that the cost of acquiring and owning the assets is higher than the profits from operating the business. For this reason, it is sometimes referred to as a 'break-up valuation'.

The Net Assets method might also be used by banks and financiers to determine a worst-case scenario for lending purposes.

Applying this valuation method to Mal's business:

Net Assets - Balance Sheet

Assets		30 June 20X0
Cash		730,000
Debtors		5,950,000
Plant	11,500,000	
Depreciation	(9,500,000)	2,000,000
Loans to associates (Family Trust)		550,000
TOTAL Assets		9,230,000
Liabilities		
Trade creditors		(3,850,000)
Hire purchase		(250,000)
Bank loans		(850,000)
Net assets		4,280,000
Owners' equity		
Accumulated profits	4,130,000	
Share capital	150,000	
		4,280,000

A word of caution on the use of this method: it may in fact result in a significant under-valuation or over-valuation of the business, depending on the accounting assumptions that have been adopted *when preparing the business' balance sheet.*

For example, the historical cost assumption (or written down values) when applied to assets may result in a significant under-valuation of the business. On the other hand, valuations ascribed to 'purchased intangible assets' (such as patents) may result in a significant over-valuation of the business.

This method is often used where the business is relatively new and is not yet generating profits or revenue. The value is based on what it would **cost** another person to develop what you have built from scratch. Such costs might include buying or developing equipment, recruiting key staff, developing the product, attracting initial customers, developing the brand, testing and accreditation.

This method also considers the **value of time** and the benefit of getting to where the business owner is immediately, as opposed to having to painstakingly work through a prolonged development cycle, which has many unique risks associated with it.

While other valuation methods may result in higher values being attributed to the business, the Build Value method often works to build a solid foundation under other valuation assertions.

Comparing different valuation methods

Comparing valuations derived from different methods can be quite informative, and a useful crosscheck of your business' value. If one method reveals a higher valuation than another, then it may reveal something about your business.

For example:

- If the valuation derived using the Discounted Cash Flow method is greater than the valuation derived using the Earnings Multiple method, then it might imply you have been through a **phase of investment** that will mean your business is expected to **substantially increase profits in the future**.

- If the valuation derived using the Net Asset value is greater than the valuation using the Earning Multiple method, it might imply that your business is either **over-capitalised or underperforming**.

- If a valuation using an Income Approach is less than a valuation using an Earnings Multiple method, it might imply that your business is either **overvalued**, or an **industry leader**.

A word about goodwill

Goodwill is often misunderstood. Goodwill is the difference between the full market value of your business as a going concern, and the value of the net assets that enable your business to continue to operate.

The accounting definition expresses goodwill as:

Goodwill = Enterprise Market Value - Identifiable Net Assets

Goodwill may or may not be transferred when a business is purchased, since it can be derived from physical factors (e.g. a location), or from personal factors (e.g. the owner's reputation or relationships with customers and suppliers).

Goodwill appears on your Balance Sheet as an asset if you have acquired a business and a value has been attributed to goodwill. This is referred to as 'acquired or purchased goodwill'. However, goodwill generally does not appear on the Balance Sheet of a business that 'created' the goodwill from scratch. This is referred to as 'internally generated goodwill'. The presence or absence of goodwill on your Balance Sheet can materially impact the reliability of your Net Asset valuation.

A common error in business valuations

A common error when valuing a business is to **combine elements of different valuation methods** – which produces a nonsense figure.

For example, it would be incorrect to take the value derived from an Income Approach method, and then *add* the value of the business' Net Assets. The value of the Net Assets has already been incorporated in the valuation derived from the Income Approach method, because those assets are required (and used) to produce those earnings. When your entity is being valued, it should only be necessary to add back net *'surplus' or 'non-operational'* assets, if any.

Case Study

In Mal's case, the Income Approaches come up with a value of around $8 million, whereas the Net Asset approach comes up with a figure of around $4 million.

It would be incorrect for Mal to simply add $8 million to $4 million and end up with a valuation of $12 million!

Calculating the 'net amount' you will be left with

The sale price you receive is just the beginning. To make the right decision about if, when and what to sell, you need to understand how much you will be left with. To arrive at this amount, you need to adjust the sale price for other **residual obligations** and **liabilities** that will reduce the net amount in your pocket.

Settling your debts and liabilities

The buyer is unlikely to assume responsibility for repaying any **debt** you have used to fund your business. The buyer is also likely to require you to transfer title to plant and equipment free and clear of any chattel **mortgages** and **finance leases**.

As the seller you will typically only be left with the 'net equity' in these assets, after the repayment of your debts. If the buyer does assume some of your debt obligations (e.g. acquires plant subject to an existing lease), then the price they pay will be adjusted downwards to reflect the debt obligation they are taking on, leaving you with the lower net amount.

Satisfying staff redundancy payments

If the buyer does not retain all your staff, then as the seller you will need to calculate, and satisfy, all **accrued entitlements** and **redundancy payments** for anyone made redundant at the time of sale.

It is also quite common to adjust the **sale price downwards** to reflect the value of the accrued entitlements of the employees being transferred to the buyer, calculated up to the closing of the sale. This is because these accrued entitlements represent an historical 'expense' from an earlier period in which you received the associated income and profits.

Employees and their entitlements are discussed in more detail later.

Settling all associated tax liabilities

The issue of tax is usually a big one. Part of your planning process will involve structuring the transaction to minimise the amount of tax arising from the sale – as this will improve the net amount left in your pocket.

The decision to either sell the underlying **assets** (and be left with the business entity), or for you to sell the **business entity** itself, is likely to have a material impact on the tax outcome.

When calculating what you will be left with, you will need to have a clear idea of the tax that will be triggered by the sale. We discuss this in more detail later.

Sharing the sale proceeds with other stakeholders

Do any third parties have a legitimate claim over a portion of the sale proceeds? If you have **business partners**, then you will be sharing the cash in proportion to your respective equity holdings.

Have you committed to pay **key employees** a bonus when the business is sold? It is quite common for owners to promise a sale bonus to keep key employees around and working hard until the sale is complete.

If you inherited the business, are any **family members** entitled (legally or morally) to a slice of the pie?

Satisfying any 'claw back,' warranty and indemnity claims

No doubt you will be required to make 'promises' to the buyer about the state and nature of the business they are buying. These are called 'representations', 'warranties', 'covenants' and 'indemnities'.

If it turns out that a promise about something is incorrect, or incapable of being performed, then you will be required to pay a portion of the sale price back to the buyer. This contingent liability can last for years after the settlement and have a material impact on what you are ultimately left with.

Participating in earn-outs

A portion of the sale price may be held back and only paid if the business meets certain targets post-sale. This arrangement is called an 'earn-out'.

Business owners often **overestimate what they will receive** from earn-out agreements. Rarely have we seen earn-out payments made without dispute.

In the buyer's mind, whether justified (or reasonable) or not, anything over and above what is paid at settlement is not considered due unless the business proves to be wildly successful, and even then, they may still hold out on later payments.

It is critical that the earn-out language be crystal clear, as any **ambiguity will lead to dispute**. Furthermore, it is prudent to base the earn-out on some objective measure of performance that is difficult for the buyer to manipulate. For example, 'gross' revenues as opposed to 'net' profit. Even if the measure is defined clearly, it can be difficult to calculate after your business has been integrated into the buyer's other operations.

Finally, if the earn-out amount is fixed or capped, you should ask for the deferred part of the consideration to be paid to an independent third party on settlement, who holds the amount as 'stakeholder' in a similar way to a deposit. If the earn-out conditions are met, then the amount can be released to you. If structured in this manner, you are much more likely to receive it. Obviously, the buyer will resist this strategy.

Collecting on vendor finance

If you agree to provide the buyer with some level of 'vendor finance' to facilitate the purchase of your business, on settlement you will move from being a business 'owner' to a business 'funder.'

The risks of lending money include the borrower dragging their feet making interest and principal repayments, or ultimately going broke.

To encourage timely repayment, you should always impose a level of **interest** that is slightly above commercial rates. Interest-free, or discounted, vendor finance is usually a bad idea.

You should also seek **security** over the business assets to back up the loan. As a practical matter, this is likely to rank after senior bank debt the buyer raises to pay any cash portion of the purchase price. Ideally you should get a **personal guarantee** from the individuals behind the buyer, but this may be difficult to negotiate when you are the seller.

Complying with any commercial restraints

A commercial restraint, or restraint of trade, will prevent you from earning income from a defined activity, for a certain period, and within a geographical location.

A restraint of this nature is like any other **liability or cost**, and your **reduced income-earning capacity** needs to be fully reflected in the 'goodwill' value of your business. We have seen people 'give away' a business for its net assets and still agree to a restraint of trade. This is akin to receiving 'negative' value for your business.

Maximising your net cash-in-hand

Once all **residual obligations and liabilities** (contingent and otherwise) have been identified and considered, you can then attempt to structure the sale to maximise your net cash-in-hand.

Case Study

Mal has $850,000 of bank debt in BTL Pty Ltd that is secured against the business' assets. This will need to be repaid out of the sale consideration on completion.

Two of the trucks are leased, with total residual balances of around $250,000.

He also has $600,000 of bank debt (in the Family Trust) secured against the Sydney depot and $550,000 has been lent from BTL Pty Ltd to the Family Trust. These debts are left over from when Mal bought out his brother John in 2005.

Staff entitlements currently stand at around $480,000 before redundancy payments. Several of the staff have been around since when Mal's father owned the business, and any redundancy payment or purchase price adjustment is likely to be high.

James has been promised a bonus of 10% of the sale price if the business sells for more than $7 million, provided James agrees to stay employed by the new owner. Mal did not realise at the time that this was 10% of the entire gross price, not just the amount above $7 million, and would be calculated before considering any liabilities left for Mal to pay out of the proceeds!

Mal will need to give the buyer a reasonable restraint of trade, which is likely to be around 3 years (if we assume that he is going to get around 3 times earnings for the business). Based on a market annual salary of $180,000 per annum, this equates to an opportunity cost of around $540,000 in lost future earnings.

If we assume a business value of say $8 million, this will be reduced by around $2.2 million of 'hard' liabilities, leaving $5.8 million, before providing anything for James' bonus, or considering the value of the restraint.

At this stage we have not considered the value of the Sydney depot – which the Council values at around $3.5 million. Given that market rent has been factored into the business valuation, it is reasonable to assume that this is not part of the sale. Mal will retain the Sydney depot and earn a healthy rent.

It is also not clear whether the bonus payable to James includes the value of the Sydney depot. Mal's strong view is that the depot is excluded, and the issue is irrelevant if the depot is not sold as part of the deal. James sees the depot as a core asset of the business, and should be included in any value, even if Mal keeps it. This is why it is critical to be precise when making promises to employees and business partners!

What to sell and what to keep

An important question that is often overlooked is whether the maximum value can be extracted by selling the whole business to one buyer, or whether more value can be achieved by either:

- Splitting your business into parts and selling those parts to different buyers; or

- Selling part of your business and keeping the balance.

What can you sell?

To start with, you need a clear picture of all the assets you **can** sell (practically), verses all the assets that **should** be sold (to realise maximum value).

For example, it may not be possible to assign a lease or a franchise agreement, which may significantly impair the value of your overall business. The same applies to 'distribution rights' you may hold that are not assignable, or at least not assignable without the supplier's consent.

Another scenario that often arises is where the seller wants to keep some key intellectual property or real estate, and only sell the 'operations'. In realty, no serious buyer will be interested in the operations of the business without the upside and strategic value of the IP or property. When you do the analysis, the value of selling both assets to the same buyer may be higher than selling them separately, (potentially at different times). But this is not always the case.

Identifying the appropriate category of buyer

There are various broad **categories of potential buyers**, and each category has a '**price range**' that they are likely to be able to afford.

For example, an employee looking to 'buy a job' may be able to afford up to a couple of hundred thousand dollars. A small business entrepreneur may be able to afford up to several million. A medium sized enterprise or private equity investor may be able to fund up to tens of millions. Whereas a listed company may be expected to have almost unlimited funds.

You will need to **target the appropriate category of buyer**, with reference to the expected value of your business. There is no point trying to sell your business to several key employees if they have limited funds and your business is worth $50 million.

If you fall between two potential categories of buyer, or you cannot get interest from the most appropriate category of buyer, then you will need to consider more creative strategies. For example, if your business is too valuable for the likely category of buyer, you will need to consider splitting your business into parts, and thereby accommodating the target categories of potential buyers who can afford to do a deal.

On the other hand, if your business is not large enough to attract the interest of the best category of buyer, then you will need to consider 'rolling up' your business with other complimentary businesses to get to a size that will attract the right level of attention.

Selling to more than one buyer

Trying to sell to more than one buyer will significantly increase the complexity of the sale. It may be that you need to sell in a series of transactions (i.e. one after the other), rather than trying to do multiple deals simultaneously (i.e. all at once).

Not all aspects of your business will be of the same **commercial character**. For example, an investment in your business operations is of a completely different nature to an investment in a commercial property used by your business. The same applies to stock, debtors, equipment and IP. Each has a different commercial value and risk profile.

To extract the maximum value for the parts of your business, you need to identify the category of buyer (or investor) for whom the particular asset best fits. For example, you may choose to sell your operations to a young and energetic entrepreneur looking to build equity value fast, and the associated real estate to an older investor looking for consistent yield and modest capital growth.

Keeping part of your business

If may be that you are not able to identify potential buyers for all the parts of your business. In this case, keeping part of your business is a common strategy to improve the affordability for the potential buyers that you have identified. In fact, you may prefer to hold on to certain aspects of your business as they will provide a better return than you could get from simply investing the cash proceeds from a sale.

Most sellers will be looking to offload the riskier and 'operationally intensive' elements of their business, i.e. the 'business operations'. However, retaining the stock for a period, and providing it to the buyer to sell on your behalf on consignment provides the buyer with a form of 'secured finance' to help them close the deal.

You may also wish to retain the real estate associated with the business and earn a market rental. If you are the buyer of the business, we recommend you get a 'first option' to acquire the real estate, particularly if this is a strategic asset for the business.

What else can you 'sell' that may be of value?

Your commercial focus as a seller should be on identifying ways to maximize value. To this end you should consider what else you can offer the buyer to make the overall purchase more attractive. This is where you can get imaginative and create further value out of thin air.

For example, you can agree to **continue working** in your business for a period after its sale. In many instances, the buyer will place a material value on this undertaking, particularly if the business is currently tied to your personal goodwill, or if the business involves technical processes and know-how that will take some time to master.

As discussed in more detail later, another thing you can offer the buyer is a strong and enduring '**restraint of trade**', so the buyer has no concerns about you competing with them in the future.

Another source of potential value for a buyer is entry into a trade association, social circle or club. Similarly, introductions to key people or enterprises within your industry or among clients.

The common element to these 'intangible' offerings is that they either **reduce the perceived risks** to the buyer (ameliorating their fears), or they **heighten the perceived upside** (stoking their greed). Use your imagination!

Case Study

There are many aspects to Mal's business that he can play with. There are the business operations, including his three key clients. There are the hard assets in the form of the prime movers and rolling stock. There is also the real property in the form of the Sydney depot.

Mal is happy to keep the Sydney depot and lease it back to the buyer for a commercial rent. Commercial property rents are generally higher than residential rents and other passive investments, and the site also has potential future development potential.

Mal is also happy to hold on to some of the hard assets of the business and lease them to the new operator. If the buyer ended up failing in the business, Mal feels comfortable that he could step back in and operate the business long enough to offload the hard assets for a reasonable residual value.

Theoretically, Mal could also retain the 'operations' and associated goodwill, and lease or license this to the 'buyer', but this would really be akin to Mal just keeping the whole business and running it under management.

As a minimum, Mal wants the incoming buyer to pay something material for the business operations and goodwill. Ideally, the buyer would also acquire all (or a majority) of the plant and hard assets.

As part of his discussions with James about James possibly acquiring an interest in the business, Mal has promised to sponsor James to become a member of Mal's golf club where he regularly meets with several of the business' key clients. James is keen to move into this circle of influence.

6

Getting Into Shape

The reality is that most businesses are not in tip-top shape 100% of the time. It takes that extra drive to get things looking their best.

Just like you would 'style' your home before putting it on the market, the same applies to your business. There is a recipe for this that you need to follow to maximise the sale price.

Your business will not have a single sale price. It will fall within a **range of potential prices**. This range can be very wide. What end of this price range you ultimately sell for will come down to how well you have minimised the buyer's '**uncertainty**' and stoked their '**greed**'.

The other thing uncertainty impacts is the **time** it will take to complete the sale process. The less confident the buyer is, the deeper their due diligence investigations will need to be, and the more carefully they will negotiate the warranties and indemnities.

In summary, you must understand and appreciate the following 'Sale Formula':

Tidy up your inventory

Your business' inventory is a common place where things can get tardy. Taking the time to tidy this up will result in a higher sale price and better sale terms.

You should make an extra effort to sell stock that has been hanging around for a long period, even if you need to heavily discount. While the profit margin on such items may be lower than regularly priced items:

- Your cash-flow will improve;

- Your revenue numbers will improve;

- You are likely to generate at least some measure of profit which will contribute to your valuation numbers; and

- The amount the buyer needs to raise will be lower.

This will also reduce the risk you assume when you give warranties to the buyer about the salability (or obsolescence) of your stock. We have seen instances where sellers have warranted that all stock is salable and not obsolete, only to later get hit with a bill for stock that had to be discounted by the buyer due to its age, *even though very little value was placed on it in the context of the sale*. So not only did the seller not get the cash for these items on or prior to the sale, they ended up paying cash back to the buyer after the event.

Case Study

Mal has a massive inventory of spare parts that he and his father have collected over the decades. Every now and then one of these parts comes in handy, but most of this stock is outdated and will never be used in the business.

On the other hand, Mal is confident that he could sell a lot of these parts to enthusiasts and tinkerers through various online forums for a sizable amount of cash.

Rather than leaving all these parts as part of the business sale, Mal and his wife have agreed to realise these assets for spare cash over the coming months.

Streamline your plant and equipment

A buyer is likely to value your business on an 'income basis', not a 'net asset' basis, (unless your business is doing poorly and is not being sold on a going concern basis). Therefore, the net book value of your plant is unlikely to have either a negative or positive impact on the sale price. Put another way, a buyer is not going to pay you more to buy plant that is *surplus to operational requirements*. A buyer will see this surplus plant as a free 'bonus'.

Accordingly, you should only offer the buyer the plant and equipment required for continued operations, and everything else (that is all surplus or idle assets) should be disposed of by you, prior to putting your business on the market. This surplus cash will go straight into your pocket and will not impact the sale price.

This will also reduce the risk you assume when you give warranties to the buyer about the operational status of your plant and equipment. We have seen instances where sellers have warranted that all plant and equipment is in 'good working order', only to later get hit with a bill to repair an asset that was not being used when the business was sold – and for which the seller did not receive any consideration as part of the sale.

Case Study

In addition to his fabulous collection of spare parts, Mal has also ended up with a wide range of rolling stock in the form of flatbed trailers, dry van trailers, refrigerated trailers, lowboy trailers and step-deck trailers. Most of the contracts only require the use of the core rolling stock, and the balance of these trailers remain in the yards and are only used occasionally.

Mal also has a couple of prime movers that are probably past their 'prime' and require a lot of maintenance. These would be better sold off to a smaller operator who has the time and inclination to keep them maintained and on the road.

Overall, Mal has identified prime movers and rolling stock with a market value of almost $1 million that he considers surplus to his core business, and that could be sold off independently of the business.

He and James also discuss the fact that they make a small loss on some of the 'specialised' freight operations using the less common rolling stock, and that getting rid of these assets and focusing on their core operations is likely to have an overall positive impact on the bottom line.

Educate your employees and facilitate their buy-in

Many people take the approach of hiding their intention to sell their business from their employees for as long as possible. No doubt they fear their best employees will be destabilised and leave – negatively impacting the value of the business.

Given the value of many businesses is heavily dependent on the quality and longevity of their workforce, managing the transition to new ownership for these stakeholders is critical.

Building and maintaining a strong enterprise culture and workforce depends on a high level of mutual trust. Surprises of any sort have an immediate and negative impact on trust. Accordingly, nothing should come as a surprise to your team.

Once you have made a definitive decision to sell your business, the best course of action is to **fully inform employees**, reassuring them of their future, and encouraging them to use the sale as an opportunity to advance their careers and further entrench themselves in your business' operations.

As part of this process, you should review staff performance, update your terms of employment and policies, and review remuneration levels to market.

As noted later, employees are also a key source of potential 'buyers' for your business. If they feel they have not been given a fair opportunity to participate in the purchase, they are more likely to sabotage the sale and then leave.

The reality is that employees will very quickly realise that you are preparing for a sale. If you leave them out of the process, they are more likely to be planning their exit than working with you to achieve a great outcome.

Case Study

Mal decides to communicate his intentions to sell the business on several levels.

He holds a series of detailed talks with James and his other senior team members, to provide them with a complete understanding of his plans and motivations, and to give them an opportunity to get involved and benefit from the transition.

Mal also prepares a high-level summary of his objectives to distribute to all staff, which will be followed up with a meeting at each location, where questions can be asked.

An open communication policy will avoid gossip and damaging uncertainty. It also makes the plan 'real' for Mal, who is now publicly committed to this course of action.

Clean up your facilities

You would think that this doesn't need to be said, but unfortunately, it does. **First impressions count – a lot!**

A clean and elegant office premises, an organised and orderly looking factory, a tidy and efficient warehouse – will make the difference between being at the lower end of the valuation range and being at the top end.

De-clutter your offices, throw out any old equipment, clean your windows, sell your scrap steel pile, paint your walls, steam clean your parking area. You get the idea.

Case Study

BTL is not known for its 'pristine' depots. Over the decades Mal and his father have taken the approach that 'you never know when you're going to need that piece of RHS steel truss'.

Mal has delegated the clean-up of the facilities to Mel, who is much less emotionally invested in Mal's collections of useful spares and equipment.

To incentivise the team to participate in the clean-up, Mal and Mel have agreed that any net money raised from selling the excess equipment and scrap will be invested directly back in the team.

Ensure your leases are in order

You are unlikely to own outright everything you will be trying to sell. For example, if you lease an office, shop, venue, factory, warehouse, or depot, make sure the paperwork is in order.

In some instances, for example a hotel sale, the lease will be the primary asset you are disposing of. In other circumstances, for example when you are being bought by a competitor with existing facilities, the lease can be a 'liability' that needs to be managed as well as possible.

Ideally, you will have a short period remaining on the existing term of your lease (to give the buyer the flexibility to consolidate with their other facilities), but also have several options to renew on market terms, if the buyer wants to stay. In fact, the expiry date of your lease may be a key factor in the timing of your transaction.

You need to carefully review your lease documentation, make sure it is signed and current, and that you have complied with all the covenants. You are also likely to need the landlord's consent to a transfer of the lease, or a transfer of the entity through which you hold the lease. It is a good idea to start this conversation with the landlord early, so it does not cause any unnecessary delays.

Case Study

Mal's Family Trust owns the Sydney depot which is BTL's main property. There was an old lease put in place when Mal and his brother bought the depot off their father back in 1997. However, the lease has not been updated since. Mal is happy to put a lease in place between his Family Trust and BTL Pty Ltd (or the buyer's own legal entity).

The two other locations used by BTL in Melbourne and Newcastle are shared space with unrelated parties. This arrangement was done on a handshake by Mal, and it is not clear if the other parties would honour the deal if someone else took over BTL.

Alex owns a depot in Melbourne, and if he sells his business to BTL, or combines it in some other way, he is happy to enter a formal lease over this property with BTL. Alex's property would be a suitable replacement to the location currently used by BTL in Melbourne.

With regards to Newcastle, Mal will either need to formalise an arrangement with the other tenant or find a suitable replacement location.

Document your key business relationships

The last thing you want in the middle of selling your business is to open major negations with one or more of your key suppliers or customers. They will see that you are in a weak and vulnerable position and likely take full advantage.

To avoid this squeeze, take the time to get all your key contracts up to date and within terms, well prior to commencing and announcing the formal sale process.

Lockdown your intellectual property

It goes without saying that an increasing proportion of business value now takes the form of intangible **intellectual property**. This includes things like your brand (such as trademarks and livery), patents, designs, copyright in code and images, confidential information (such as client lists) and knowhow (such as service and industrial processes).

There are ways to maximise the protection afforded to these assets. Some intellectual property can be registered with government agencies, including trademarks, patents, industrial designs and recipes. While other IP can be protected through contracts with relevant persons, such as the creator of copyright, or persons to whom confidential information or processes are divulged.

A buyer paying full value will take the time to thoroughly review the extent to which you have protected, and can pass on the full benefits of, these assets.

Case Study

BTL has been trading under the name 'Been There Logistics' for decades but has never officially registered the name and logo as a trademark. More recently, the team and customers have also been referring to the business by its acronym 'BTL'.

To avoid any suggestion that the buyer will not be able to confidentially take over and trade under this name, James has been tasked with registering the trademark with IP Australia.

BTL also has a couple of other names that are associated with some profitable specialised transport operations, which will also be registered as trademarks.

Ensure your financials are up to date

It is amazing how many people start a sale process with incomplete or out-of-date financials. This is complete folly.

Before even thinking about selling your business you must have both:

- Audited **financial statements** for the most recently completed three financial years; and

- Accurate **management accounts** that can be prepared up to the present day.

Most small and even medium sized businesses will balk at the concept of having their accounts audited. This is an expensive and time-consuming exercise. The short answer is that if your business is being sold for anything north of $5 million, you will more than recover the cost of a formal audit of your accounts for the immediately preceding three years. There will be plenty of people who ignore this advice, but it pays.

If you do not have an accounting system that can provide accurate and complete management accounts up to the present day, then you need to get this in place before thinking about selling. You simply cannot go into a sale process without accurate and timely accounting information.

Furthermore, you should not be relying on your external accountant for this information. Your business needs to have the capacity to produce this information daily without external input. Your accountant can assist you to put systems in place to do this, but they should not be responsible for running the system. There is nothing more disconcerting than a prospective buyer requesting some current piece of financial information, only to be told that the seller has requested their external accountant to prepare it.

Build a credible alternative

You will not be able to sell your business for its inherent value without true **competitive tension**. Unfortunately, for many businesses there is likely to be only one or two genuine potential buyers. Creating and maintaining competitive tension in this scenario can be difficult.

The only way to guarantee competitive tension for your sale is to create your own genuine and credible alternative to a sale – namely to **retain your business** and run it under **professional management**.

For this alternative to be credible, you need to start building the infrastructure for this option as soon as possible. This means promoting key employees within your team into more senior management roles, or if that is not possible, hiring professional management externally. It also involves building and documenting durable business systems.

The reality is that you are unlikely to earn the same amount from investing the proceeds from selling your business in more traditional investments like bank deposits, investment property or listed shares. So, the option of spending some of your 'profits' on quality management, able to run your business for you, is a truly credible alternative to selling

Case Study

As we work through the issues of valuation and discuss the level of returns Mal is likely to make from investing the net sale proceeds, Mal is becoming more attuned to the idea of retaining at least some of the business and investing in filling-out his management team.

Mal has great faith in James' ability to manage the business, and if he acquires or 'merges' with the operations run by Ken, the business will have someone who is good with the numbers and systems (James), and someone who knows transport and logistics from the ground up (Ken). Mal is also still quite young, and he can remain on the board and get involved in interesting projects from time to time.

If Mal is happy to retain a significant equity interest in the business, then he is more likely to get a top price as he sells down his equity over time to his growing management team.

Furthermore, once greater depth is established in the management team, it is more likely that an external 'professional investor' will get involved and pay an even a higher multiple for the whole business.

'Asset Sale' versus 'Entity Sale'

Most businesses are run through a **legal entity**, such as a company, or trust. When it comes to selling you have a choice of either:

- The entity selling the underlying **business assets**: an '**Asset Sale**'; or

- The owners of the entity selling the **legal entity itself**: an '**Entity Sale**'.

This is not always an easy decision, and often becomes a point of negotiation between you and the buyer.

Asset Sale

In an Asset Sale, the entity through which you operate the business transfers title to the **business assets** used in the business to the buyer, i.e. the underlying property, plant, equipment, IP, etc.

From a buyer's perspective, an Asset Sale is viewed as 'clean', in the sense that it poses a **lower tax and liability risk** to the buyer. The buyer takes over the business assets and leaves the historical trading risks and liabilities in the legal entity that you retain. The buyer can perform a few statutory searches to ensure that **title to the assets** is clean. Other than that, there is little for the buyer to check.

As the seller, Asset Sales can be harder to manage from a tax perspective. First, the sale price needs to be apportioned among the various assets sold, and this can give rise to taxable *balancing charges*.[5] Furthermore, the entity may not qualify for the general 50% ***discount capital gains***,[6] and it can be more difficult accessing ***the CGT small business relief***.[7] It is safe to say that in most instances, an Asset Sale will result in more tax for the seller.

If the business is **'contract intensive'**, then the seller and buyer will need to procure a transfer or novation of these contracts from the selling entity to the buyer's entity. This can take time and lead to negotiations with third parties. In an Asset Sale the employees will also need to be moved between legal entities.

An Asset Sale will require a detailed consideration of Goods and Services Tax (GST) and stamp duty consequences.

Entity (or share) Sale

An Entity Sale (or share sale) involves you transferring ownership of your **legal entity** to the buyer, that in turn brings with it the underlying business assets.

Generally, an Entity Sale is more complex to document and implement. This is because the 'net position' of the thing being sold (i.e. the legal entity) changes daily up to the time of transfer. These transactions also involve a higher level of **due diligence**, and more comprehensive **warranties and indemnities**.

There are circumstances where an Entity Sale might be preferred by both parties. For example, where it is easier to sell shares than it is to assign or novate many contracts, leases, licenses and employees.

From a buyer's perspective, Entity Sales are viewed as 'dirtier', in the sense that they pose a **higher risk of unforeseen liabilities**. This is because the legal entity, along with its historical encumbrances and liabilities, pass to the buyer.

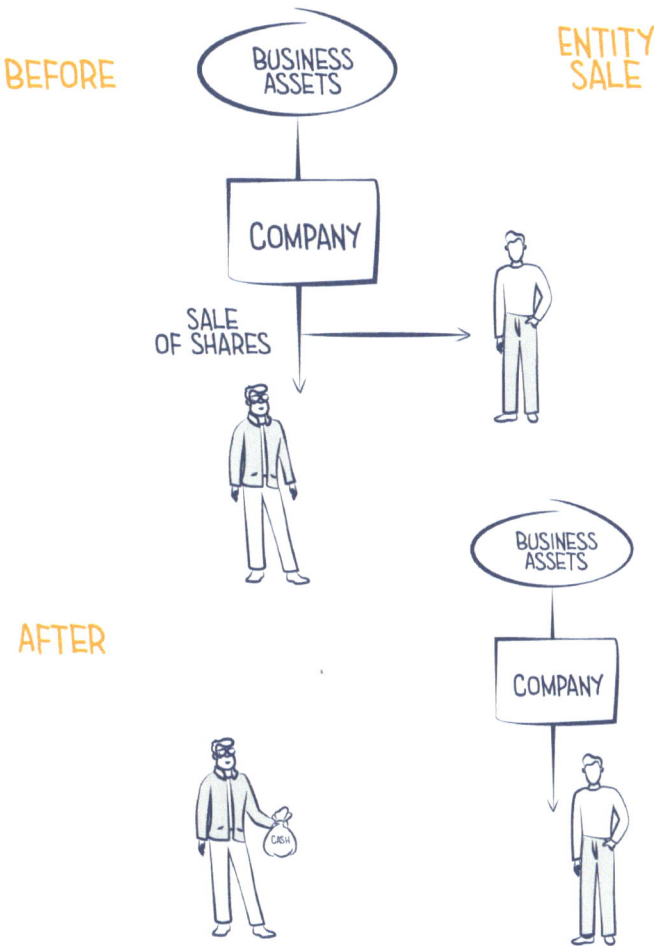

BEFORE

BUSINESS ASSETS

COMPANY

SALE OF SHARES

ENTITY SALE

AFTER

BUSINESS ASSETS

COMPANY

CASH

To mitigate this additional risk, a buyer will typically require more comprehensive warranties and indemnities from the seller. The buyer will also require much more information about the entity and its historical dealings before concluding the deal.

Buyers in Entity Sales typically incur **higher transaction costs**, because of the additional due diligence required to detect potential liabilities attached to the transferring entity, and to document appropriate protections.

From the seller's perspective, an Entity Sale will usually result in **capital treatment for tax purposes**, which is likely to result in a lower overall tax impost. But the news is not all good; if the entity needs to be restructured prior to the sale, for example if non-core assets need to be moved out of the entity, then this is likely to trigger additional tax.

Generally, a large corporate buyer is more likely to be able to handle an Entity Purchase. Whereas, a small private buyer is likely to insist on an Asset Purchase.

Case Study

Mal operates the business and holds the business assets through three entities: BTL Pty Ltd, BTL Holdings and his Family Trust. It would be possible for him to sell both BTL Pty Ltd and BTL Holdings because they are both companies. However, his Family Trust is an 'unfixed' discretionary trust, which is not capable of being 'sold'.

If Mal can attract a large corporate buyer, or if he elects to sell down equity to his management team, then he is likely to be able to sell the *shares* in BTL Pty Ltd and BTL Holdings.

However, if he is only able to sell to another small businessperson, they are likely to insist on an *Asset Sale*, given the very long trading history of Mal's two companies, and the potential liabilities associated with the transport industry.

It may be that an Entity Sale is very favourable to Mal from a tax perspective, in which case he may even be prepared to offer the business to his management team for a relatively lower price, because of the tax savings associated with an Entity Sale.

Pre-sale structuring and restructuring

Regardless of whether an Asset Sale or Entity Sale is pursued, as a seller you should use the pre-sale period for streamlining and restructuring operations and assets to achieve the best outcome.

As referenced earlier, this process may include divesting surplus or idle assets, acquiring additional (complimentary) assets or businesses, segregating and separating assets that are to be retained, distributing profits and capital to stakeholders, and ensuring that liabilities and encumbrances that will not pass to the buyer are satisfied or extinguished in full.

Be aware that some pre-sale restructuring can have significant tax implications. Furthermore, if the restructure results in a 'tax benefit', then the Tax Office may seek to negate this benefit if the restructure is seen as artificial or contrived. For this reason, it is important to undertake any restructuring as early as possible, and ideally years before an actual sale is concluded. Obviously, this will not always be possible, but if you are just embarking on the sale journey, then a good place to start is a conversation with your accountant and tax lawyer.

Case Study

James' long-term friend and corporate adviser, Edward, is keen to make an investment in an active business like BTL. Edward is also optimistic about being able to attract a syndicate of high-net-worth individuals to invest alongside him. However, Edward wants to ensure that the business is not too heavily reliant on Mal as the founder.

James and Edward have also been progressing discussions with Ken and Alex about combining all three businesses to create a bigger 'roll-up' opportunity to invest in. Having Ken involved alongside James would alleviate some of Edward's concerns about placing too much reliance on Mal.

So far, Ken has agreed to combine his business with BTL in exchange for an on-going equity stake in the combined businesses, provided both businesses are valued on the same basis, and some level of 'blue-sky' value is ascribed to his patents.

Alex, who is Mal's age, is keen to sell his business for cash, but it prepared to remain active in the business and provide a level of secured vendor finance for a limited period of time.

Getting paid

Stating the obvious, as a seller you should give serious thought to how you would like to be paid, and when. Surprisingly, many sellers often assume that buyers are willing and able to pay the full purchase price at settlement. However, buyers often wish to explore alternatives, such as payment of the purchase price by instalments, retention amounts, earn-outs, and financing options such as 'vendor finance'.

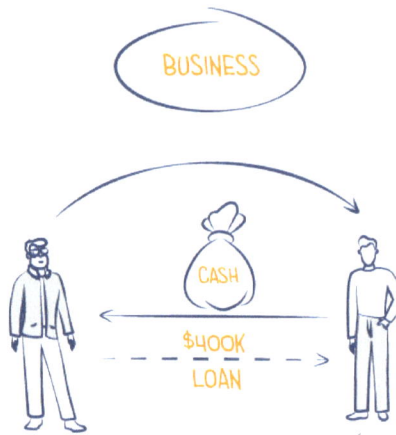

Vendor finance is provided when the seller agrees to defer receiving a portion of the purchase price, and instead recognises a loan owing from the buyer to the seller as from settlement of the sale. Vendor finance is considered in more detail later in the sections dealing with buyer strategy.

You should spend some time formulating a clear and confident position on your **payment preferences** at the beginning of the sale process. If you are prepared to offer some level of vendor finance, then we suggest this be proffered early in the negotiations, as it may increase competitive tension and the final price achieved. You should also specify the level of security that you will require for the vendor finance, so this can be factored in when the buyer is organising their bank funding.

Case Study

Mal is realistic and understands that the value of his business is too expensive for someone looking to 'buy a job', but not large enough to immediately attract a professional investor who is able to pay the full value up-front.

Mal is therefore willing to explore a staggered 'sell-down' of the business, as well as providing a level of 'vendor finance' to the buyer.

With respect to the deal that James and Edward are formulating, they suggest that Mal may wish to retain some 'equity' in the business going forward. This will provide Mal with the opportunity to share in the up-side from rolling-up Alex and Ken's businesses.

Mal is less keen on this option, because he can see that there is increased up-side from combining the three businesses. However, he can also see risk in merging and then operating the three businesses as a single unit.

7

Steps in the Sale Process

When you have carefully addressed each of the pre-sale considerations, your attention must then turn to the **formal sales process**. Once again, proper planning will facilitate effective execution.

Developing a robust and disciplined **sale strategy** should be a part of your planning process. Your sale strategy should 'demand' that a prospective **buyer works hard**. This is because the most likely buyers of your business are your competitors and existing employees, (and existing employees can quickly become competitors). The last thing you want is to allow competitors and employees who are not genuinely interested in purchasing your business to have a 'free look' at your confidential information.

As such, depending on how competitive the market is for your business, you can use one or all the following sale steps to **'filter' genuinely interested parties** from those just looking to acquire commercially valuable information.[8]

Steps in the sale process

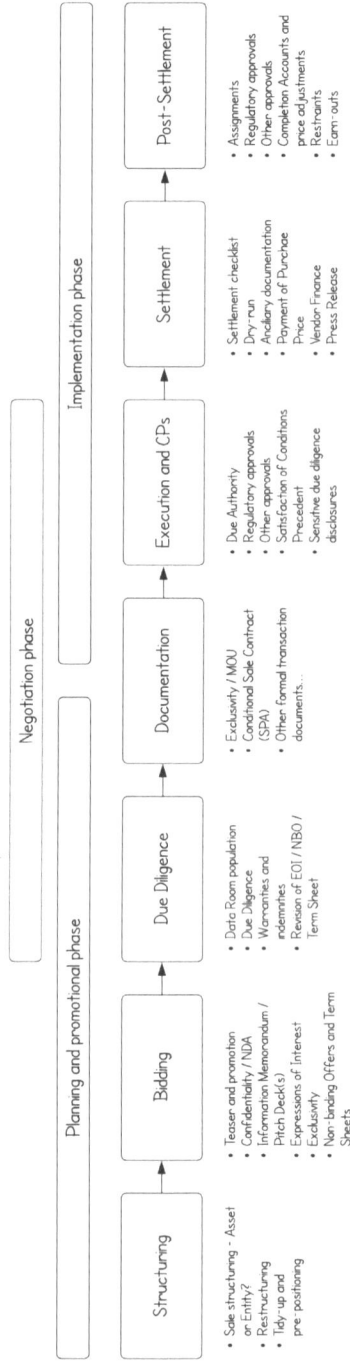

Planning and promotional phase

Negotiation phase

Implementation phase

| Structuring | → | Bidding | → | Due Diligence | → | Documentation | → | Execution and CPs | → | Settlement | → | Post-Settlement |

Structuring
- Sale structuring - Asset or Entity?
- Restructuring
- Tidy-up and pre-positioning

Bidding
- Teaser and promotion
- Confidentiality / NDA
- Information Memorandum / Pitch Deck(s)
- Expressions of Interest
- Exclusivity
- Non-binding Offers and Term Sheets

Due Diligence
- Data Room population
- Due Diligence
- Warranties and indemnities
- Revision of EOI / NBO / Term Sheet

Documentation
- Exclusivity / MOU
- Conditional Sale Contract (SPA)
- Other formal transaction documents...

Execution and CPs
- Due Authority
- Regulatory approvals
- Other approvals
- Satisfaction of Conditions Precedent
- Sensitive due diligence disclosures

Settlement
- Settlement checklist
- Dry-run
- Ancillary documentation
- Payment of Purchase Price
- Vendor Finance
- Press Release

Post-Settlement
- Assignments
- Regulatory approvals
- Other approvals
- Completion Accounts and price adjustments
- Restraints
- Earn-outs

Filtering-out the tyre-kickers

You want prospective buyers who are genuinely interested in exploring your business to **become 'invested' in the sale process**. This investment will take the form of **time**, **money**, and most importantly, **emotion**.

The more **disciplined**, **robust** and **fast-paced** your sale process is, the greater the opportunity to pre-qualify genuine buyers. Once a party has become invested in the process, by engaging people like lawyers, accountants, financial advisers, valuers, bankers and insurance agents, they will have demonstrated a genuine interest *through their actions*.

Another aspect of a robust and disciplined sale strategy is for you to meet early and regularly with both your managers and advisers, i.e. your 'Deal Team'. Their feedback and support for your sale process is critical, because when deal fatigue or distraction become an issue for you (and they will), managers and advisers will play a key supportive role, ensuring that momentum is not lost.

Managers and advisers will also help to formulate the path forward – addressing threshold questions such as:

- ☑ What is the proposed timetable for the sale process?

- ☑ Who has responsibility for what during each step in the sale process?

We now discuss the key steps in a robust and disciplined sale process.

The 'Teaser'

The Teaser is a short one- or two-page document that provides a very clear but **high-level overview of your business** and invites interested parties to enter into a **Non-Disclosure Agreement** (**NDA**) and request an **Information Memorandum** (**IM**).

What is the purpose of the Teaser?

The purpose of the Teaser is to ensure that <u>**all**</u> potential buyers are made aware of the fact that your business is for sale. For this reason, the Teaser must be disseminated as far and wide as possible.

Who should receive the Teaser?

As many people as humanly possible.

So many sellers are concerned about too many people finding out they are trying to sell their business. This reluctance to promote the sale often results in a compromised sale process and a low sale price.

If you are pushing back on the idea of widely distributing your Teaser, then you need to go back and re-do the **Reality Check** discussed earlier, because chances are you are not yet fully committed to the sale process.

Are you worried about too many people finding out about the sale?

Quite often sellers are concerned about too many people becoming aware of the impending sale too early in the process. You may be concerned about customers or clients hearing about the sale and asking what's going on. You may also be concerned about employees becoming aware. As already noted, it is our view that management should inform employees of a potential sale as early as possible, so that they can control the information flow, and avoid it becoming a subject of gossip.

To mitigate these issues, some sellers elect for a third party to disseminate the Teaser document, and your details can then be omitted from the Teaser, i.e. a 'Blind Teaser'. This third party could be your accountant, lawyer, broker, financial adviser, or all of them. They then act as the first point of contact for requests for the Information Memorandum (the **IM**). Of course, in certain industries competitors may be able to guess who is selling just based on the high-level information in the Teaser.

Where does the information come from?

From a practical perspective, the Teaser is usually put together *after* the IM has been prepared. Having the IM complete will mean all the relevant information is at your fingertips, and a good summary in a 'marketing' format can be prepared in the form of the Teaser.

Advertising and promotion

A key recurring theme in this book is the importance of creating and maintaining **competitive tension** during the sale process. The advertising and promotion part of the sale process is critical to achieving this.

Beware advisers who don't value competitive tension

While it may sound counter-intuitive to some, do not engage the services of a broker or other expert if they express any of the following (flawed) views:

"I have a buyer on my books who is perfect for this business."

"We can save money on advertising by approaching a buyer I know directly."

Why is this strategy bad? Such a strategy does the direct opposite of creating competitive tension – it limits **the target market** to one buyer, which is a recipe for disaster, (from your perspective, as seller).

"There is no need for advertising or marketing or promotion (or an open house, in the real estate context), because we have a pre-vetted group of buyers that we should first approach directly."

Why is this strategy bad? Every business is unique and different, and no broker or adviser who has just been introduced to the business knows enough about it to **limit the target market** by concluding promotion is not necessary.

The reason brokers make these suggestions is that they know you will want to limit the breadth of people to whom you expose your business. This is a very natural tendency, but you need to strongly resist this tendency if you want to get the **best price** in the **shortest possible time**.

Like most things, timing is critical. Starting promotion as early as possible after getting sale-ready will give you the greatest chance of realising maximum value for your business.

In what ways is your business unique?

Emphasising the **uniqueness** of your business is a key part of effectively promoting your business. Perhaps it occupies a unique niche in the market, maybe your staff have unique skills and experience, or perhaps you are solving an issue or providing a product or service in a unique way.

The uniqueness of your business needs to be highlighted. Through the marketing process all prospective buyers need to be educated on precisely how your business is unique and thus *valuable*.

Involve all your advisers

You should inform all your advisers of your decision to sell your business as early as possible in the sale process. Advisers know a **broad network of people**, many of whom you may not be aware of, and so this serves the purpose of immediately broadening your prospective market.

Involving your advisers also gives them an opportunity to expose and introduce your business, which they should know well, to their other clients and industry contacts. This will give your advisers an opportunity to be involved in the value-creation process, for your business, for their own practices, as well as for the businesses of their other clients. It is an all-around win-win scenario.

Going on a 'roadshow'

Roadshows are a useful tool for marketing your business. While many business owners have not been through the process before, many of their advisers have (or should have!) – and their experience and expertise in this area should be leveraged.

You will need a '**Pitch Deck**' of slides for this purpose. How to prepare a Pitch Deck is discussed later.

Where are you likely to find your buyer?

Advertising, promotion and marketing are all for one key purpose: finding a buyer willing and able to purchase your business for its maximum realisable value.

Buyers come from a variety of 'sources' and a well-executed marketing strategy will reach each source, including:

- ☑ Family and existing staff.

- ☑ Competitors wanting to reduce competition.

- ☑ Other competitors wanting to expand horizontally.

- ☑ Suppliers wanting to move up or down the supply chain.

- ☑ Retirees wanting to invest surplus funds in a stable operating business.

- ☑ 'Job' seekers who have decided they might wish to be self-employed.

☑ Migrants, looking to provide a means to support their families and themselves.

☑ Professionals seeking a 'lifestyle' change.

Although brokers may promise you a 'list of interested persons', this rarely turns out to be true. As soon as you appoint a broker, they will turn-around and ask you who you think is the most likely buyer – including who are your competitors, suppliers and customers.

The reality is that *you* are the most reliable source of a list of persons most likely to purchase your business. You just need to ask yourself the right questions!

No matter what the nature of your business, one of the key aspects of executing a successful sale is to get the message out to as many potential buyers as humanly possible. This is not a time to keep your light under a bushel.

Professional investors

Depending on the size of your business, and what industry you operate in, you may be able to attract the attention of professional investors. These take several forms, including:

- Experienced 'angel' investors;

- Private equity funds; and

- Venture capital funds.

Private equity

Private equity investors generally invest in **established businesses**. They back an individual or management team to take an existing business to the next level of growth. They may do this in the context of an industry 'roll-up', where they put several businesses together to create a larger enterprise capable of listing on a public market.

This strategy may consist of an **industry consolidation** play, where they put together several competing businesses, or a vertical integration play where they put together several businesses along a **horizontal supply chain**.

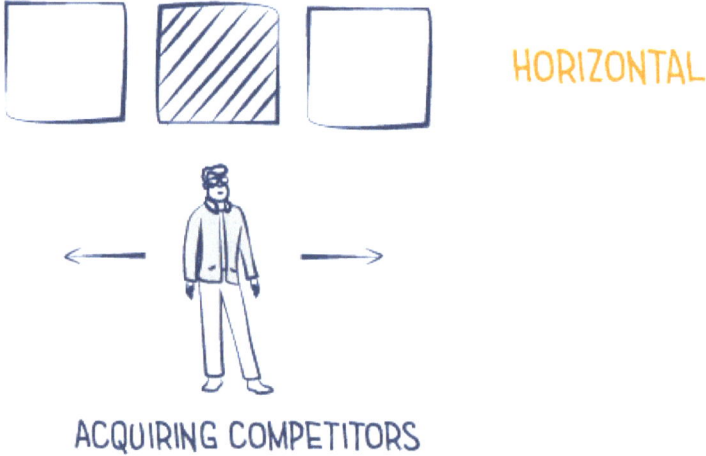

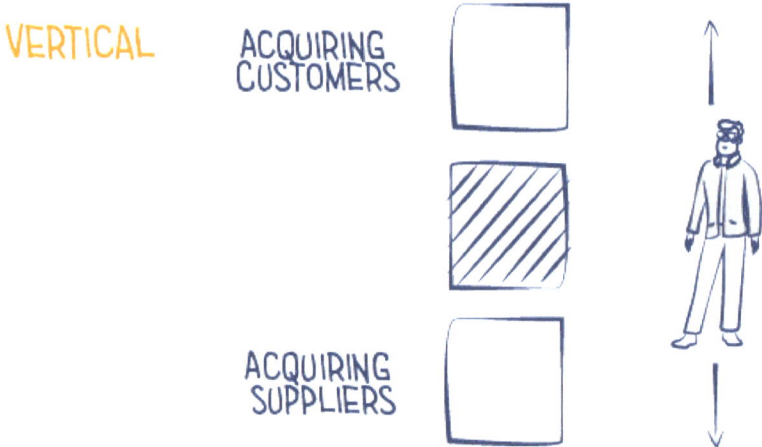

HORIZONTAL

ACQUIRING COMPETITORS

VERTICAL

ACQUIRING CUSTOMERS

ACQUIRING SUPPLIERS

Case Study

In Mal's case, he may be able to attract the interest of a private equity investor to fund the acquisition of the two competitors (owned by Ken and Alex) to form a larger company to move forward with under the stewardship of the younger management team (led by James and Ken).

By bringing in a professional investor or syndicate, Mal is more likely to be able to take some cash 'off the table', as the younger managers are less likely to have significant surplus cash to invest themselves.

When professional investors come into a business like this, they usually do so by providing cash in the form of 'preferential' equity and debt. This then leaves a larger portion of ordinary equity to be divided among the management team.

If things go well, the private equity investor and the management team all do well.

If things don't go well, the preferential rights held by the private equity investor will give them effective control over the business so they can then minimise their downside.

Venture capital

Venture capitalists generally invest in **early stage** or high growth enterprises. In many ways, private equity and venture capital are indistinguishable. However, venture capitalists tend to invest longer term equity to develop new income streams, whereas private equity providers tend to employ a high amount of leverage (or preferential debt) to financially engineer an increase in value from existing assets and income streams.

A further category of professional investor is an **angel investor**. These investors will typically invest in the combination of a business and an entrepreneur or management team. The angel investor will be looking to back you (or your management team), which is likely to require you to stay around for an extended period.

Case Study

If Mal retains a material ownership interest in the business, but steps back and lets James and Ken take a more active role in running the business, Mal will effectively transition from an 'owner-operator' to something more akin to an 'angel' investor. Mal will be backing the new management team to take the business forward, and maintain and increase the value of the equity that he leaves in the business.

Similarly, Edward may lead an 'investor syndicate' to provide the cash to buy a controlling stake in BTL from Mal, as well as provide cash to acquire Alex's business outright. This syndicate would effectively be backing James and Ken (and their executive team) to take the combined businesses to the next level.

Selling to family

If you are planning to sell your business to a family member, then good luck! We have almost never seen this done successfully.

There is a long list of likely issues with this strategy, including:

- A lack of ability for them to raise the necessary money, hence you end up acting as their bank;

- A lack of respect for the true value of your business, because they believe they have helped you create the value; and

- An expectation that you will 'look after them' by selling cheap and stepping back in if things go bad.

But perhaps the biggest downside to selling to family is the 'perpetual guarantee' that you will end up providing to them. This guarantee goes something like this:

> *"If at any time and for any reason the business*
> *doesn't end up hugely successful, then it is all*
> *your fault, and you will do whatever is necessary*
> *to make sure I never lose any money...."*

If at any time in the future you do not honour this guarantee, then your family relationships will be forever damaged.

We are not saying you should not look to family members to *take over* your business, but if you do involve family members, understand that this is a family '**succession strategy**', and not a commercial 'sale strategy'.

Selling down to employees

Selling to one or more key employees can be a realistic exit option. However, there are many similarities to selling to family. In short, you are **unlikely to get the best possible price for your business**, and you will **retain a material level of responsibility** for the ongoing success of the enterprise.

The mindset of an employee is monumentally different to that of an entrepreneur. If someone has been a solid and long-term employee, chances are they are not fired by the entrepreneurial spirit. This is in no way a criticism, merely a factual observation. Some people do not want the 14-hour days with no mental break for the next two decades of their life. The life of an entrepreneur is inherently single-minded (and even 'unbalanced'). Not everyone shares these priorities.

While your employees may covert your seemingly 'free' lifestyle and material success, few will really be willing to make the necessary sacrifices, and even fewer will be willing to acknowledge your earlier sacrifices. So, when you invite them into the world of equity ownership, they are likely to come with a degree of 'entitlement'. If you can live with the fact that they will expect (and likely get) an easier ride than you had, then selling to employees is a worthy strategy.

If you do go down this path, you need to identify employees who are well-rounded, and not just great at their existing job. They need the technical, professional and emotional maturity to buy-in and tuff-it-out over the long term. Running a business is a 'generalist' pursuit and does not suit a 'specialist' mentality.

Case Study

Mal has considered the potential pros and cons of involving James as an owner in the business. Ideally, he would sell out completely to James (and possibly Edward as a co-investor alongside James).

However, Mal realises that if he involves James as a buyer, he will need to have some level of continuing association with the business. This will take the form of a continuing equity stake while James buys-in over time, or as a debt funder providing a material amount of vendor finance. In either case, Mal is likely to continue to shoulder a significant degree of financial responsibility for the business for many years ahead.

Mal prefers the concept of selling out completely, to either an arm's length buyer, or to a consortium of management, third party professional investors, and competitors, in the context of a merger/roll-up.

However, Mal is prepared to enter a transaction consisting of:

- The sale of a controlling stake in BTL for a combination of cash, vendor finance on commercial terms and shares;

- The roll-up of BTL with Ken and Alex's businesses, with the senior management team consisting of James and Ken;
- The involvement of an investment syndicate led by Edward to provide both cash and preferential debt to the combined businesses; and
- The retention by Mal of a material equity stake in the combined businesses, with the first option to sell-down equity if others want to take it up.

Managing the communication process

Many people think that selling their business will be 'negative' news for clients, customers, employees and suppliers. But this is simply not the case.

Disclosing the fact that you are selling can represent a risk, but only if you let other people take control of the narrative, such as competitors, or if you leave it up to the gossip mill. Therefore, it is essential to get on the front foot and **take proactive control of the communication process**.

In fact, your customers may already be concerned about your age and be wondering who is going to take over the business should something happen to you. By selling to a larger company, or to a younger management team, you may allay their fears. The same applies to employees who are looking for a secure and prosperous future beyond your tenure. They should be the first people to know of your intentions, and why your decision is a good thing for them.

Non-Disclosure Agreements

Before an interested party is given access to detailed information about your business, they should be required to sign a legally binding Non-Disclosure Agreement (**NDA**).

What is the purpose of an NDA?

The purpose of an NDA is to:

- **Restrict the parties who gain access to your confidential and commercially sensitive information** to those who you agree to deal with as part of the sales process. An NDA will prevent them from passing on the information to third parties (other than their advisers); and

- **Restrict what the recipients can do with the information you provide them**. This is usually limited to the purpose of evaluating the potential purchase of your business – as opposed to using the information to compete with you or poach your employees.

What if someone refuses to sign an NDA?

Some professional investors and larger enterprises resist signing NDAs. In fact, this has become a bit of a trend among venture capitalists and private equity investors.

The basis for this refusal is hard to articulate but is usually because the party already holds equity in other similar businesses or is looking to invest in other similar businesses in the future. The investor does not want to hamper their existing or future activities by signing an NDA.

In short, you should **simply not engage further** with prospective buyers or investors who take this approach. This is because their justifications for refusing to sign an NDA do not hold up to logical scrutiny.

An NDA will only protect confidential information that is **unique to you**, and therefore it would be totally inappropriate for a professional investor or large enterprise to use this information in the context of another business they already hold an investment in, or in a business they may own in the future. *They are in no different a position to one of your competitors who is looking to acquire your business.*

It is not a good sign if a prospect refuses to sign a well drafted and balanced NDA. Don't waste any further time with them, things will only get worse as the deal progresses...

⬡

Case Study

Mal insists that each of the parties involved in the roll-up and sell-down enter *mutual NDAs* to protect their respective confidential information from unfair use.

This includes James, Edward, Ken and Alex, as well as the members of the investment syndicate led by Edward who will receive any information provided during due diligence about any of the three businesses.

Mal insists that James also signs an NDA even though he is currently employed in the business and is subject to the confidentiality clauses of his employment contract. This is because James is not acting in his capacity as an employee when it comes to buying a stake in the business, and James is likely to be privy to more extensive and sensitive information that he would ordinarily see as an employee.

The Information Memorandum

The information memorandum (**IM**) is a critical document, and you will not be able to realise the maximum value for your business without a properly drafted IM.

What is the purpose of the IM?

The purpose of the IM is to provide potential buyers with the information they need to **assess whether they are interested in acquiring your business**, and if so, **whether they can afford it**. In short, the purpose of the IM is to answer a buyer's obvious questions about your business.

Where do you get the information to prepare the IM?

Many existing businesses already have a Business Plan, Strategic Plan and Marketing Plan, which should contain information that can be re-purposed as a good starting point for your IM.

A small number of highly sophisticated entrepreneurs (having a clear focus on 'exit') have valuations and their IM updated periodically, such as every quarter or year – even when they are not actively selling. This is how they run and continually benchmark the performance of their business as they build it to a point when it can be sold to professional investors or listed on a public equity market. When it comes time to sell, they have a road-tested and up-to-date IM ready to go.

Most businesses will not have an up-to-date IM or plan, and will therefore need to gather the required information and data from their business systems. The raw data will then need some massaging to get it in a form where it can **answer the obvious questions that buyers will want answered**.

Extracting data and preparing the IM will take time and resources and can become a distraction for your team. You need to plan for this and start as early as possible. (It will only get worse during the due diligence phase...)

What information should be included?

Typical IMs cover several areas, and should be:

- Helpful and informative to prospective buyers; and

- Protective of you, the seller, through disclaimers and disclosures.

IMs typical take the following format:

☑ An overview of the **key aspects of your business**.

☑ A summary of the key characteristics of the **market you operate in**.

☑ A description of the **assets you are selling**.

☑ A summary of **financial information** that conveys the core financial drivers of your business.

☑ An overview of the **key strategic value** of your business, as well as any obvious future potential.

☑ The **steps in the sale process** that potential buyers must follow.

☑ A **timeframe** for completion of the sale transaction.

☑ An **Expression of Interest** form that an interested party can fill out to indicate they wish to be part of the sale process.

The IM should also include appropriate legal **disclaimers** and **statutory disclosures**.

Many states compel statutory disclosures of certain information relating to small business sales and/or sales involving real estate.[9] These disclosures need to be provided in a **prescribed format**. The prescribed format does not match the format of a well drafted IM. It is common for these disclosures to be provided separately to the IM (or as an appendix to the IM).

If there is a strong possibility that foreign buyers may be interested in your business, then *Foreign Investment Review Board* ('FIRB') disclosures and information will need to be considered.[10] This is usually dealt with at a later stage in the sale process after the buyer characteristics have been determined.

If the business entity is listed on a public market (e.g. the Australian Stock Exchange (ASX)), then continuous disclosure obligations and change-of-control issues will need to be considered.

Should you include an indication of price in the IM?

It is not easy to decide whether to nominate a price, or price range, in the IM.

Some traditional negotiators will tell you there is a benefit to 'anchoring' the price towards the higher end of your anticipated range. However, more contemporary negotiation methods suggest that if the market in which you are selling is 'shallow' (i.e. the market price range is not well known), then a more effective strategy is to **go last on price**, i.e. to let the buyers go first.[11] Generally, the real market for your unique business is unlikely to be 'deep' and well established, so the second strategy is likely to be the most effective.

By letting the buyers go first on the question of value, they will need to base their bid on the *value to them*, which may be considerably higher than what you are expecting. This may include some component of **strategic value** or **synergistic value** they place on your business – which may not necessarily be reflected in the wider market (or in your view of what your business is worth).

A prospective buyer is unlikely to have a clear insight into the competitive landscape for your business, and if they are interested, then they are likely to provide you with an accurate and honest view of the value they place on your business.

Case Study

A traditional valuation of Mal's business would reference the recurring adjusted 'net profits' generated. However, if a competitor acquired the business, they may be able to reduce costs by combining various back-office and infrastructure costs (e.g. administration, depots and maintenance departments). The buyer may therefore be willing to value Mal's business on a 'marginal revenue' basis, rather than a net profits basis.

Another possibility is that a competitor has freight routes that are complimentary to Mal's routes. For example, Mal has a large client who mainly moves cargo from Sydney to Melbourne, and his trucks often return part full. A competitor with a client with cargo travelling in the opposite direction would be able to combine with Mal's business to achieve overall higher efficiencies for both operations.

In the context of Mal selling into a roll-up with Ken and Alex's businesses, there is likely to be significant synergistic value created by the transaction that can be shared between the participants. This would include a rationalisation of back-office overhead, rolling-stock and depots, access to better economies of scale, as well as the ability to rationalise freight routes and improve overall utilisation.

If Mal gives his indication of value early, then he may miss the chance to share in the additional value that a particular buyer or transaction places on his business. Alternatively, if Mal can create and maintain competitive tension, as well as control the transaction structure, he is more likely to end up capturing a disproportionate share of this additional value.

For these reasons, we recommend against the IM disclosing an expected value or price range. In fact, we recommend you require a potential buyer to provide an **indication of the value range** at which they would be prepared to transact, as a 'gate' to the next stage of the sale process. Genuinely interested parties will take the time to make their own assessment of the likely value of your business. Whereas tyre-kickers will usually drop out at this stage. Put simply, there is little downside to asking the buyers to go first on price.

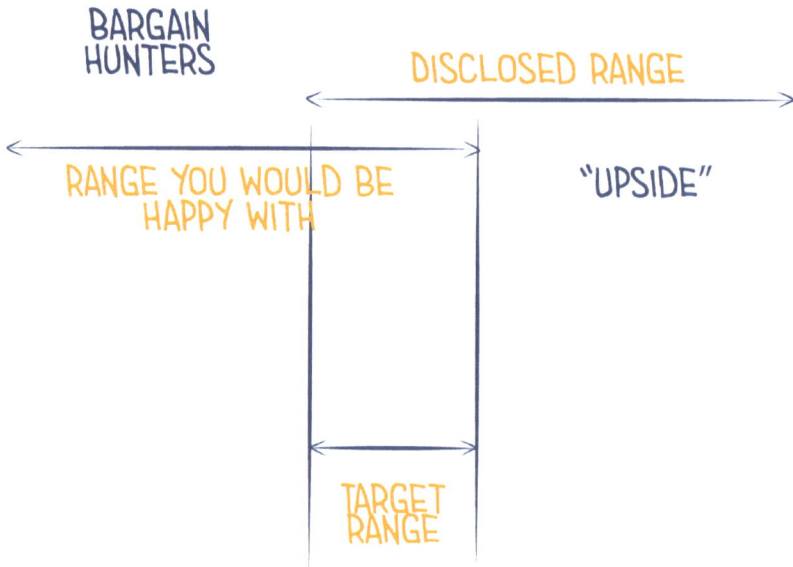

BARGAIN
HUNTERS

DISCLOSED RANGE

RANGE YOU WOULD BE
HAPPY WITH

"UPSIDE"

TARGET
RANGE

If a buyer refuses to provide an indication of price, and you still want to move forward with them, then you can consider referencing a **broad range of prices** within which 'similar businesses' have been sold. You should anchor the lower end of the range at the top of what you would be prepared to accept, with the higher end of the range extending well beyond what you are hoping for – to leave room for the buyer to identify strategic value.

Maintaining control over the sale process

One of the most important themes that should emerge from preparation of the IM is that you, as seller, must always **retain control of the sale process**.

Once a prospective buyer seizes control of the process, the chances of a sale at full market value are severely compromised. (In fact, the chances of concluding a sale at all may be compromised.) This is true both in terms of how and when the information is presented, as well as how accommodating you are to a prospective buyer's demands.

Some suggested strategies to ensure you retain control of the sale process include:

☑ Begin by using the 'Teaser'. This will ensure that you get the **maximum possible interest** from potential buyers. You simply must build **competitive tension** to sell your business.

☑ When a prospective buyer asks for an IM or additional information, you should require the buyer to sign an **NDA** as a condition to receive any detailed information. This typically forces (serious) prospective buyers to engage a lawyer to review the NDA, which means they are now starting to become 'invested' in the process. For this reason, we recommend a relatively long and complex NDA, rather than a short and simple one.

☑ You should be very conscious of your words and actions, and especially conscious of how accommodating you are to prospective buyer demands. You need to accommodate their requests, but in the context of you **running a process** that feels like there are multiple parties. You need to exude just a little bit of indifference, while continuing to push a fast-paced sale process.

For example, if a prospective buyer demands that you deliver a certain document or information at a certain time, even if it is readily available, you should promptly respond that the information will be made available at a later point in time, and to *all* the interested parties at once. This may sound petty, and like we are suggesting you 'play games'. That's because we are.

How much information is enough?

Prospective buyers will **not** need information about the identity of your key clients and suppliers to make an accurate assessment of value or a decision to proceed with a purchase of your business.

However, prospective buyers will need **aggregated data**, such as your total revenue, broken down between key product and service lines. They may also need some aggregated data about the **profile** of your customers.

Prospective buyers will **not** need to know who your employees are. However, they will need to know what **capability** you have on staff. They may also need to know if these people are committed to staying on, and what their key employment terms and entitlements are.

If you release too much information at the IM stage you can **damage the end value of your business**, because a potential buyer will know that if they are successful in acquiring your business, then their future competitors are also likely to have that information from the sale process.

You cannot take back information, so if in doubt, leave it out. You should seek advice about the **extent of your disclosures**, particularly if you are dealing with current or future competitors, (which you should be!).

On the other hand, you need to accept that the more information you disclose, the more likely you are to attract potential buyers. So, you need to strike a balance between saying enough to get people interested, but not saying so much that you devalue your business by providing competitors with commercially sensitive data. An experienced adviser will be able to help you tread this delicate line.

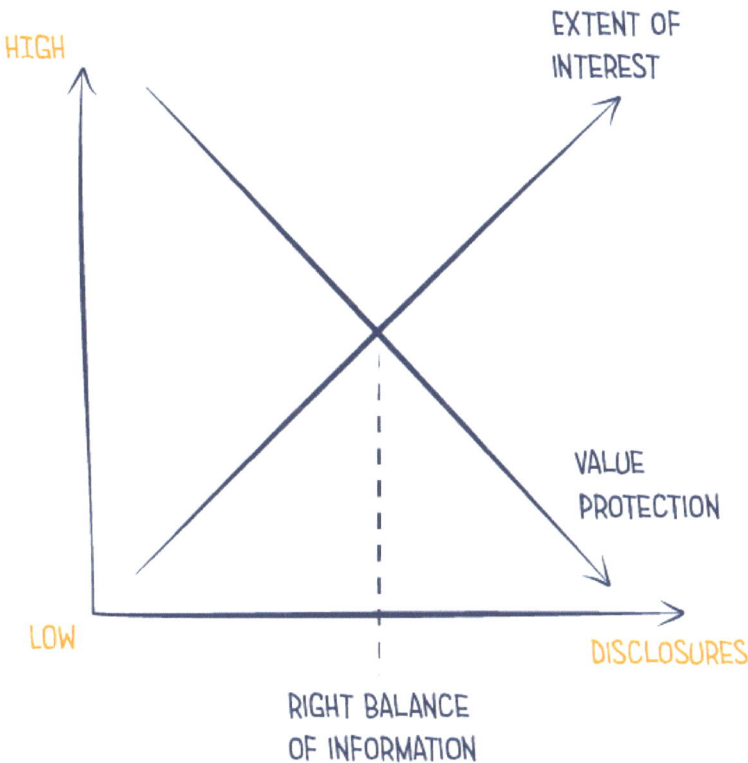

The Pitch Deck

The Pitch Deck is something that falls part way between the Teaser and the IM. Essentially, it is a set of slides that can be used to efficiently convey the critical elements of the IM and summary data to potential buyers, (and other people involved in the sale and purchase, including senior employees, bankers, and insurers).

When preparing the Pitch Deck, you should you assume you are going to present it to a Board of Directors. You are doing more than just selling the deal (*a la* the Teaser), but you only have a limited time to convey the **critical details** of the proposed deal.

Some advisers have taken the approach of replacing the IM with the Pitch Deck. We still believe both documents are necessary, because combining them into one document results in either an IM that is too short and lacking necessary detail, or a Pitch Deck that is too long for its intended purpose - to efficiently convey key information and 'sell' the deal. In fact, you may end up with several different pitch decks, each aimed at a different audience.

Expressions of Interest

The IM should invite expressions of interest (**EOIs**) from interested parties.

It is important to once again highlight the importance of you, as seller, to maintain control during this stage of the process. You should provide a **standard format** in which prospective buyers must reply to elicit the relevant information you need to assess their suitability to move forward in your sale process.

You should set a hard and fast **date** for receipt of EOIs. The EOI should require an indicative price range from the interested party, a requirement that the interested party specify the nature and extent of data they will require during their due diligence phase, and inviting them to make any other unsolicited comments.

You and your advisers will then need to review the EOIs to identify any genuinely interested parties.

Some important questions you will be looking to answer from the EOIs and conducting buyer due diligence include:

- ☑ Can the buyer get the necessary **funding**?

- ☑ Does the buyer have the necessary **qualifications** and **experience** to run the business?

- ☑ Will it be difficult for the buyer to get the necessary consents, **licenses** or approvals?

- ☑ Does the buyer have a clearly defined **plan** for the future of the business?

- ☑ Will existing customers 'approve' of, or be comfortable dealing with the buyer?

- ☑ What are the EOIs telling you, the seller? That is, what useful feedback do the EOIs provide that you were not expecting? Are there any opportunities in this information?

- ☑ Is there a consistent (or inconsistent) 'theme' in the EOIs, and what does that theme tell you, as seller?

Case Study

Initially Mal got 16 enquires to receive an IM from interested parties. Some of these were large national transport companies, while others were from people with small operations that Mal was already familiar with. This initial level of enquiry made Mal feel quite good about the process.

However, as the deadline to receive Expressions of Interest (EOIs) grew near, Mal had not yet received a single response. He really wanted to go back to the people who had asked for an IM and give them more time to respond and provide an EOI. He also wanted to reduce the amount of information they needed to provide in their EOI response. This is a common reaction.

But the sale process is a filter. If a party does not have the time or interest to give the acquisition some thought, and properly respond with a formal EOI, then they are never going to go all the way through with an acquisition at a reasonable market price.

The reality is that there are probably only one, or possibly two external parties who, at the time you want to sell, have the energy and inclination to seriously consider buying your business. It is better that Mal comes to terms with this now, rather than after he has disclosed commercially sensitive information to a broad range of tyre-kickers.

On the final day of the EOI process Mal received a detailed EOI from a national transport operator looking to acquire incremental revenue on the freight routes services by BTL, as well acquire Mal's unique portfolio of specialised rolling stock. Mal now has two options to move forward with, the roll-up by the management team, and a straight sale to this national operator.

Non-Binding Offers or Term Sheets

Once a universe of genuine prospective buyers has been identified (through the Teaser, preliminary IM, advertising and promotion, and review of EOIs) (the **Short List**), a more detailed IM, or an **additional set of disclosures**, can be circulated to the Short List of interested parties, for the purpose of them submitting **Non-Binding Offers** or entering a non-binding **Term Sheet**.

Managing further disclosure

The additional information provided to the Short List should include:

- Any **additional business information** and data not previously disclosed in the preliminary IM. This data may be in response to questions raised during the EOI process;

- The **draft Sale Contract** (being an Business Sale Agreement or Share Purchase Agreement, as you deem applicable);

- A draft **Due Diligence Index** summarising the information and access that will be provided to parties undertaking due diligence enquiries; and

- An **invitation** to the Short List to submit **Non-binding Offers**.

During this next phase you (and your advisers) must continue to manage disclosure, such that:

- Data is released in stages. Only as much information (not more) as is necessary should be disclosed;

- Only **'qualified' buyers** (as identified from the EOIs and follow up discussions) are granted access to additional information;

- Everyone should receive the additional information (and any further releases) at the **same time** and be given a similar period for review; and

- Access to premises and staff should **not** be permitted at this stage. To the extent that you are providing access to information via a Data Room, this should be located at the offices of an adviser, and not on the business premises.

Further actions you require from bidders

The invitation to submit a Non-binding Offer should include the requirement for the party to provide the following:

- ☑ A **mark-up of the draft Sale Contract** with their proposed amendments and additional terms (the **Contract Amendments**). This should include any conditions precedent, additions to the warranties and indemnities, and any restraint of trade. This information will enable you to identify any 'deal breakers' from a legal standpoint.

- ☑ Confirmation of adjustments to the indicative bid price (the **Indicative Price**). This is in the context of the further data that you have provided to them, and the terms on which the deal is proposed in the draft Sale Contract.

- ☑ A list of assumptions that the prospect needs to verify during due diligence, to justify their Indicative Price (the **Key Buyer Assumptions**). This will help you efficiently manage the due diligence process.

- ☑ A checklist of information that the bidder expects to see during the due diligence process (the **Due Diligence Checklist and Questionnaire**). While this may overlap with your Due Diligence Index, it will help you prepare for the due diligence process, as well as assess the assumptions on which the bidder is basing their bid.

Providing these things will require each interested bidder to consult with their professional advisers, once again, increasing their investment in the process.

Bear in mind that you are still trying to get each prospective bidder to commit **financially** and **emotionally** to the process of buying your business. You do not want to make the process too easy. You will not scare away a *genuine* buyer through this process. (The only reason you would make the process any easier is to defer the point in time when you must confront the true extent of interest in your business.)

Many prospects will resist this, or just ignore some or all the requests, but importantly, the really interested parties will take it seriously and make this investment. The extent to which a party complies with this process will give you valuable insight into their true level of interest.

Reimbursement of bid costs

Prospective buyers may complain about the cost associated with making a complying Non-binding Offer, including the time invested, and the money spent with external advisers such as lawyers, accountants, and corporate finance executives.

If you have whittled down the prospects to two or three parties, then you may wish to encourage them to move forward by you offering to **reimburse a portion of their bid costs**, *should they be unsuccessful.* Each prospect still needs to incur the costs upfront, but they will be comforted to know that not all these costs will be thrown away should they be unsuccessful.

In fact, you can use this strategy even if there is just one genuine bidder. It can create a **real sense of competitive tension** and ensure that this party is not put-off from moving forward on your terms, purely because of the likely costs involved.

Finally, if you do offer to reimburse the costs incurred by an unsuccessful bidder, we recommend you make this conditional on the party fully complying with the steps and meeting your deadlines within the sale process. This will provide all parties with an additional incentive to **stay on your track**, and not try and take over the bid process.

The outcome from Non-binding Offers

The net effect of the Non-binding Offer process will be to **filter prospective buyers** even further. Any sensible offers, whether binding or not, will clearly demonstrate a higher level of engagement in your sale process.

It is worth recognising at this stage that requiring an NDA, EOI and Non-binding Offer from a prospective buyer is asking a lot. If a buyer is not genuinely excited about the prospect of buying your business, then they will not jump through these hoops. This is why it is critical to manage the first part of the sale process well.

The Teaser and IM need to be engaging and well-structured. The Teaser needs to be widely disseminated, and you need to openly and aggressively advertise the fact that your business is on the market. You may wish to go on a 'roadshow' with a brief Pitch Deck or hold a webinar for interested parties.

Many people avoid an appropriate investment in the initial **marketing phase** of the sale, and then try and make it up in the later stages. Their broker ends up dragging prospects through a loose and drawn-out sale process, that results in a sub-optimal outcome.

If you do not get off on the right foot, you will end up having to give away too much sensitive information to too many people in the IM and due diligence phases, only to end up with a less than optimal price.

Exclusivity

You will find that the genuine prospective buyers will seek to deal exclusivity with you as soon as possible. They will argue that this is necessary before they can justify investing significant resources in a comprehensive due diligence process and negotiation of the Sale Contract.

If someone asks to go exclusive with you, this is a good sign. It means they are genuinely interested.

Maintaining competitive tension

But there is a more important reason why a well-informed buyer will seek to deal with you exclusively. Your agreement to exclusivity with one bidder will immediately **kill competitive tension**.

As soon as you lose competitive tension, your bargaining position will be severely weakened. Other bidders will fade away, and you will be left negotiating with a single bidder who knows you now have little choice but to conclude a deal with them.

Our advice to you on the matter of exclusivity is this: **proceed with maximum caution and avoid it if at all possible**.

As noted above, one method of addressing buyers' concerns about the cost of contested bidding is to offer to cover some or all their costs if they are unsuccessful. The likely increase in sale price associated with maintaining competitive tension through due diligence (and even potentially through negotiation) will more than offset this cost.

Use multiple milestones during any exclusivity period

If you decide to offer one bidder exclusivity, you should place very clear **limits on the time** this exclusivity will last. The buyer should not just be given one final drop-dead date, but rather a series of **milestone dates** they must continue to meet to maintain exclusivity. If at any time they miss one of these milestones, you then have the option to terminate their exclusivity, and bring other prospects back into the sale process.

Case Study

Mal is keen to pursue a roll-up and sell-down involving his manager James, and the complimentary businesses owned by Ken and Alex. He is also happy for Edward to arrange funding through a syndicate of private investors.

Because Mal is dealing with a key employee and his associates, he is less concerned with the formalities of a Non-binding Offer. However, Mal still requires the bid team to provide an indicative price, the assumptions on which that price is based, a list of information they will require during due diligence, and the engagement of lawyers to prepare the roll-up and sell-down documentation.

Provided the deal team meets Mal's requirements and moves along at an agreed pace, he is prepared to deal exclusively with them at this point.

However, if Mal's milestones are not met, then he reserves the right to terminate the negotiations and go back to the national logistic company that has expressed an interest in the business.

Due Diligence Enquiries

Now that you have established which prospective buyers are genuinely interested in your business, the next stage of engagement is the due diligence process.

The role of Key Buyer Assumptions

If you have undertaken a successful Non-binding Offer process, you will have a list of the **Key Buyer Assumptions** on which the bidders have based their decision to proceed and on which their **Indicative Prices** are based.

The primary purpose of the bidder undertaking due diligence is to **validate the Key Buyer Assumptions** against actual data, and thereby justify a purchase decision at the Indicative Price.

Due diligence is not always seen in this light. Many buyers see it as an opportunity to determine if they are **really interested in buying the business**, or to **identify what may be wrong** with the business. They are also likely to see it as an opportunity to identify things that **justify lowering their Indicative Price**. If they have gained exclusivity prior to due diligence, this is also when they will have greater negotiating power to squeeze you on price and terms.

The role of the Key Buyer Assumptions is to negate this tactic, or at least negate unjustified price adjustments. If something negative is found during due diligence, but it does not undermine a Key Buyer Assumption, then there must be very good justification for the bidder to argue that it has a price impact.

The role of due diligence for the seller

From your perspective as seller, due diligence is when you get the opportunity to provide the prospective buyers with additional key or relevant information, which should help them make a **purchase decision**.

A well-executed due diligence program will allow you to communicate and substantiate the **true value** of your business. If you have nothing to hide, this is the time to prove it.

Warranties and indemnities

It is not possible to properly understand the purpose of due diligence without a clear understanding of warranties and indemnities.

Filling the gaps in due diligence

It is very hard, if not impossible, for a prospective buyer to fully acquaint themselves with all the potential upsides and pitfalls of your business in the limited time associated with the sale process.

A buyer will attempt to 'fill the gaps' in this discovery process by asking you to make **representations** and **promises** about how things have been, how things currently are, and how things are likely to be in the future. These representations are called '**warranties**'.

For example, rather than reviewing all your tax lodgements, the buyer may ask for a representation that all your lodgements are accurate and up to date (i.e. a 'tax compliance warranty').

To the extent you have disclosed material to the bidders, they will also require warranties from you promising that the information is true and complete (i.e. **disclosure warranties**). Disclosure Warranties act as an incentive for you to provide good quality information during due diligence.

In addition to warranties, the buyer may also ask you to **indemnify them** for an identifiable amount should a warranty that you have given turn out to be false, or if an identified or unaccounted for liability arises.

For example, if it transpired you had not lodged your most recent tax return and the entity the buyer purchased had an unexpected tax liability, you would need to indemnify the buyer for this additional tax.

It is generally easier for the buyer to claim a specific amount under an indemnity (e.g. the amount of tax), rather than substantiate a claim for damages for breach of warranty (i.e. the loss suffered). Often the indemnified amount and the loss suffered will be the same, but proving 'actual loss' in a warranty claim can be harder than claiming an 'identifiable amount' under an indemnity.

Due diligence v. warranties and indemnities

There is a direct **trade-off** between a comprehensive due diligence process and the need to include warranties and indemnities about factual matters in the Sale Contract.

If you provide bidders with absolutely all the information that they could possibly ask for to fully understand your business, as well as the means to independently verify your data, then there would be no need for any factual warranties and indemnities. The bidders could still justifiably ask for a **disclosure warranty** which warrants that your disclosures were true and complete, and for **specific indemnities** to cover identified liabilities.

On the other hand, if you hold back any information, because of its commercial sensitivity or because it is too expensive to provide and assess, then the buyer will expect a **factual warranty and indemnity** to protect them should your representations or promises about the fact or matter not prove to be true or complete.

Given this trade-off, the best way to avoid excessive warranties and indemnities is to provide very **comprehensive due diligence material** to the prospective buyer. However, there is a risk to this strategy. If the bidder has not yet become legally obliged to buy your business, and you expose them to every aspect of your business, including its commercially sensitive aspects, the bidder may pull out and have the benefit of that information. It is possible to manage this tension through a **two-stage due diligence process**, discussed below.

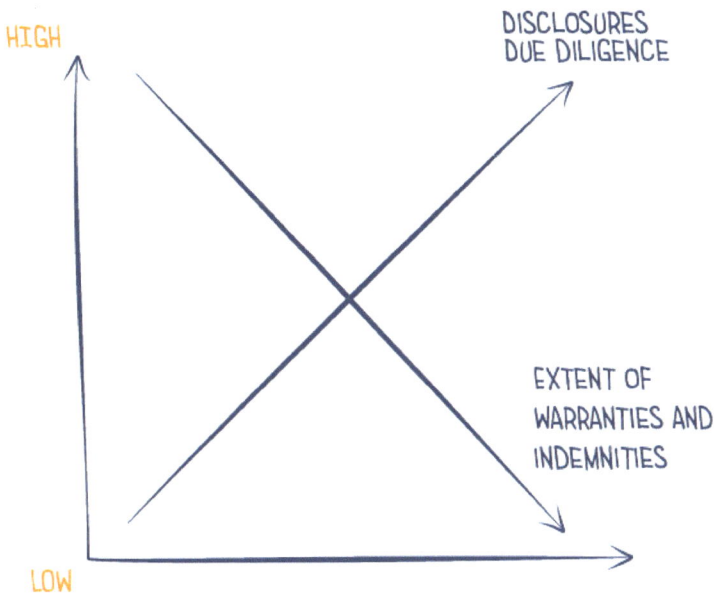

Why disclosure is better than giving a warranty

You may be wondering why you would bother with due diligence at all. Why wouldn't you just include comprehensive warranties and indemnities in the Sale Contract and move on?

The simple answer is one of **responsibility** and **interpretation**. For example, the buyer may have a concern about the condition of your stock. The buyer can either **inspect the stock** and make up their own mind about its condition and saleability, or they can **request a warranty** that you believe it is in good condition and saleable.

If the buyer inspects the stock and is satisfied, that is the end of your responsibility. If the buyer is later unable to sell the stock, it is not your problem.

Whereas, if you warrant that the stock is saleable, and the buyer is later unable to sell it, they are likely to make a claim under the warranty on the basis that you misrepresented the saleability of the stock.

There may be many reasons why the stock is not selling, but the buyer will state that you warranted it was 'saleable'. Even though you are no longer involved in the business, the responsibility still comes back to you – maybe years later.

Accordingly, due diligence **disclosures** are always **preferable** for a seller, over giving a warranty, because this ends the seller's responsibility for the matter. Incidentally, as a seller you should refuse to provide both disclosure and a warranty about the same thing. However, allowing comprehensive due diligence means that the prospective buyer will know everything about your business – so you better make sure they are locked-in to buy it!

How do warranties work?

As noted above, a **warranty** is a promise or guarantee about something. It may be a promise that something has or has not occurred, or that it may or may not occur in the future, or that something is complete, true and correct.

*For example, you may warrant that you have
not been sued for a product failure in the
past 3 years, or that you are not aware of any
circumstances that may result in you being sued
for a product failure now or in the future.*

You should avoid giving warranties about things the buyer can **verify through their own inquiries**. Due diligence is the buyer's opportunity to satisfy themselves about their concerns, and for you to minimise the extent of any warranties you are required to give to fill any disclosure gaps.

In an ideal world, due diligence should provide the buyer with the ability to personally satisfy all their enquiries and concerns. However, in the real world, it can often be easier for you to provide a warranty about something rather than all the disclosures that would be necessary for the buyer to satisfy themselves.

It is important to remember this interplay between disclosure and warranties. When negotiating whether a warranty should be included in the Sale Contract, the easiest justification for its exclusion is that relevant material was **disclosed during due diligence** for the buyer to make their own assessment, or that it is available on a public register.

Breadth of warranties

As the seller, you will want to limit the number of warranties you give and keep the wording of the warranties you provide very **specific and narrow**. In contrast, bidders will push for a comprehensive set of warranties drafted in general and broad terms.

You should avoid giving warranties along the lines that you have told the bidder everything *they need to know* to make an informed decision about buying your business. It is not your job to teach a bidder what they need to know to properly assess whether they should buy your business. This sort of warranty is far too subjective and prone to dispute.

You can also use warranties to keep certain information and details confidential until *after* a binding agreement has been signed by the buyer.

For example, you could warrant that no individual customer accounts for more than 10% of your revenue, and that they are unlikely to cease to deal with the business because of the sale. This may enable you to keep the identity of this key customer confidential until after the buyer is legally bound to acquire the company.

What happens if a warranty proves false?

If the buyer discovers that a warranty is not true, they have some options. If they discover this before settlement, they can terminate the deal. If they discover that a warranty is untrue after settlement, then they can get back some of the purchase price to compensate them for the loss or 'damage' they suffer from having relied on the false promise.

How do indemnities work?

An **indemnity** is an obligation to pay a party a specific amount if a contractually specified event occurs (or does not occur). It is usually set as a sum to be paid by one party to another party by way of compensation for the *anticipated* loss likely to be suffered should the event happen. This obligation to make the payment can arise regardless of who is responsible for the event, and without the benefited party having to prove actual loss.

In the context of a business sale, it is common for indemnities to be given to 'back up' the warranties. The relevant 'event' triggering the indemnity is a 'breach of warranty'. The specified amount is usually stated to be the loss suffered by the buyer from the breach, but it can also be stated as an identifiable or anticipated amount arising from the breach.

An indemnity may also be given to cover an amount that is known to both parties prior to signing the Sale Contract, i.e. a **specific indemnity**. A common specific indemnity is for the tax the business will be liable for in respect of the pre-settlement period.

Disclosures against warranties and indemnities

In addition to providing access to information through a due diligence process, you can also make specific '**disclosures**' against the general warranties and indemnities that provides additional information to the bidders.

It is not a matter of either giving a warranty or not giving a warranty. Often a warranty will be true, *but for* a limited number of exceptions. In this case the warranty is given, but then a specific **disclosure** is made against the warranty about the exceptions.

Case Study

One of the warranties Mal is asked to give is that: 'The business has not been involved in any litigation within the past 3 years.'

Mal discloses the dispute he had with the subcontractor who failed to properly insure his rig, including the financial cost of $65,000.

In addition, Mal was involved in a dispute with a parts supplier 3 years ago. This dispute was ultimately resolved in Mal's favour and he received a settlement of $12,000.

While this second dispute does not reflect 'negatively' on Mal's business, it is information a buyer may want to be aware of. For example, the buyer will then know to be wary about that supplier in the future.

Mal can still give the litigation warranty, but he will need to ensure he discloses details about these disputes to the buyer prior to entering into the Sale Contract.

Disclosures are another way of satisfying the buyer's requirements for information about **specific concerns**. Of course, if due diligence or disclosures confirm a concern of a buyer, they may seek to **adjust the price** they are willing to pay for your business, or require a **specific indemnity** to cover the amount.

Disclosures typically either **support** warranties or identify **exceptions to** warranties. For example, a warranty may state that all the employee entitlements due up to settlement are disclosed in a nominated schedule. The schedule of entitlements is a disclosure that *supports* the warranty. Alternatively, a warranty may state that the business has not been sued and a disclosure may provide information of a time when the business was sued. In this case the disclosure identifies an *exception* to the warranty.

The material provided to the bidder in the due diligence process is usually stated to represent a **general disclosure** against all the warranties. If there is something in the due diligence material that contradicts a warranty, then this is treated as an exception disclosure against that warranty.

In addition to this general disclosure through due diligence, **specific disclosures** are usually provided in the form of a '**disclosure letter**' that the seller gives the buyer immediately prior to signing of the Sale Contract, (including various 'drafts' prior to this event). The disclosure letter contains specific exceptions to and disclosures against the warranties.

Case Study

Following on from the example above, Mal can make disclosure of the disputes with the subcontractor and the supplier by including details of these disputes and their resolution in the Data Room that the buyer has access to during the due diligence phase. The buyer would become aware of these disputes when going through the information in the Data Room.

Alternatively, Mal could include information about the disputes in a Disclosure Letter given to the buyer prior to the buyer signing the Sale Contract.

Placing limitations on potential warranty and indemnity claims

Warranties and indemnities represent a 'long-tail' potential liability for you as the seller. There are recognised and legitimate ways to put limits on the extent of this potential liability following settlement.

In addition to making full disclosure against warranties and general indemnities, you should also look to **limit your exposure** in the following ways:

☑ Limit any actionable warranties and representations to those that have been reduced to writing and are specifically **incorporated into the sale documentation**. This will exclude any undocumented verbal representations that may have been made by your advisers and staff during the sale process.

☑ **Cap the monetary amount** that may be payable under the warranties and indemnities. This is usually limited to the amount of the sale price you have received.

☑ **Limit the time** during which a warranty or indemnity claim can be made following settlement. This is open for negotiation and can range from 6 months to 7 years. The time limit for tax claims usually matches the relevant amendment period, usually 4 years.

☑ Place a *de minimus* **amount** on the ability to make a claim, so the buyer does not make frivolous small claims. The *de minimus* will depend on the value of the business sold, and the likely cost of bringing a claim. Something like $50,000 to $100,000 is common.

☑ **Limit claims to direct losses** and specifically prevent claims for 'consequential losses'. The buyer may reasonably insist on some level of consequential loss being covered to the extent that it is reflected in the sale price.

☑ **Prevent double claims** for a breach of warranty, a claim under an indemnity, or recovery under insurance.

Depending on the circumstances, you may wish to put other more specific limitations on the warranties and indemnities.

The warranties and indemnities dance

As you can see, the issue of warranties and indemnities is a complex one, that requires careful consideration and expert advice. The due diligence process and the negotiation of warranties and indemnities is likely to take up a significant chunk of the time required to conclude the deal.

How to manage the due diligence process

Due diligence is basically an **exchange of information**. From the buyer's perspective, they will be seeking to get the best possible understanding of the risks and opportunities of your business. From a seller's perspective, it is an opportunity to disclose information that will be treated as having been disclosed against, and therefore watering-down, the warranties in the Sale Contract. It is also an opportunity for you to emphasise the quality of your business.

As the seller you should have a **standard set of due diligence material** that you propose to give to the bidders to both:

- Satisfy the bidders of their decision to proceed with the purchase of your business; and

- As disclosures against the warranties and general indemnities in the Sale Contract.

You will make this information available to each bidder, irrespective of whether they ask for it. You will have already provided a draft **Due Diligence Index** summarising this information to the bidders you have invited to make Non-binding Offers.

Part of each bidder's Non-binding Offer should include their **Due Diligence Checklist and Questionnaire**. This usually takes the form of a checklist of items they require information or answers about. It is likely to overlap with your draft Due Diligence Index.

Other than the standard disclosures you propose to make to all bidders, it should be up to each bidder to decide what additional information they require to properly assess your business. It is not your job as seller to try and double-guess what additional disclosures may be needed.

Maintaining the Data Room Index and Due Diligence Program

With this information you can prepare and maintain a **Data Room Index** that records all the data and information you have made available to the bidders. This is critical because it evidences the disclosures you are making against the warranties and general indemnities.

We strongly recommend the use of an off-site **Data Room** (on the seller side) for many reasons, including:

- ☑ By placing physical distance between the due diligence exercise and the business' location, interruptions to your business operations are minimised.

- ☑ Unintended disclosures, that can arise from unplanned or informal interactions with staff on-site, are avoided.

- ☑ Controlling access to business staff. Prospective buyers will only have access to those employees invited to the Data Room.

- ☑ Controlling what information is accessed. By keeping a detailed 'inventory' of Data Room contents, you will be able to manage what information has been shared, and with whom.

You can also prepare a **Due Diligence Program** that sets out how you are going to provide access to other resources, such as key staff and partners.

If you are engaging with more than one prospective buyer, you may need to manage this process by having the due diligence undertaken in **stages**.

Keeping a track of disclosures

It is critical that you keep a detailed inventory of the disclosures you have made to each bidder, and that this inventory is formally integrated into the sale process with appropriate references in the sale documentation. If there is a claim against a warranty or general indemnity by a buyer down the track, your first line of defence will be to argue that the buyer was made aware of the issue during due diligence, and hence the issue was subject to adequate disclosure and does not give rise to a claim.

You need to track not only the documents made available in the Data Room, but what **questions** were asked by each bidder, and your standard responses, as well as what **physical access** each bidder had to business facilities and assets.

Ideally, all additional questions from a bidder should be in writing, and then responded to in writing. It is fine to have free-flowing conversations, but the sale documentation should specifically exclude any warranty about the content of these discussions. **Anything the buyer wants to incorporate into your formal disclosures and warranties should always be reduced to writing**. This needs to be included as a specific limitation to the warranties and general indemnities.

Begin negotiation of the Sale Contract

You should begin the negotiation of the Sale Contract during the due diligence phase, paying attention to the interplay between the negotiated warranties and indemnities and the disclosures being made.

This will keep the sale process progressing, as well as further cement the bidder's commitment to a deal. In cases where you are not able to provide a meaningful response to a due diligence enquiry, you can take this into account in the wording of the warranties and indemnities.

When should bidders gain access to your physical premises?

Bidders should not be given access to your physical premises or to staff and third parties until after they have entered into a **legally binding agreement** to purchase the business, (even if only a conditional agreement). How you achieve this is discussed below. As a practical matter, they may pay a short 'visit' to your premises or facilities before this, but any time at your premises, or with your staff, should be supervised and minimised.

Protecting privacy during due diligence

Australia has increasingly comprehensive **privacy and data protection** laws at both the federal and state level.[12] You must understand how these laws apply to you and your business, and ensure that you continue to comply with these laws during the sale process.

You must ensure that any personal information and data you hold is not disclosed during due diligence, or as part of the sale process, in a manner that is inconsistent with Australia's Privacy Principles. This may include personal information about your employees, contractors and customers.

Furthermore, many of the contracts that you will have entered during the ordinary course of your business will have **confidentiality obligations**. These include contracts with suppliers, customers, joint venture partners and government departments. You may need to obtain the prior permission of the counterparty before disclosing any confidential elements of these contracts during due diligence.

Related party bidders and due diligence

Often the buyer will be someone who already has some involvement in your business, or may in fact be responsible for large areas of the business, for example, your management team. These people may know more about aspects of your business than you do. The same applies to a business partner who is looking to buy your equity in the business. This can complicate the negotiation of warranties, indemnities and disclosures.

If you are dealing with a buyer who already holds significant equity in the business, it is reasonable for the level of warranties, indemnities and disclosure to be significantly reduced. This is especially the case if the purchasing partner is actively involved in the business. You, as the seller, will need to give warranties as to **good title** of your interest in the business, and for any aspects of the operations for which you have primary responsibility. However, it is reasonable for you to resist giving warranties and indemnities about matters your business partner has primary responsibility for, or should have full knowledge about as a fellow owner.

If the buyer is a member of your management team, or maybe your entire management team, then it is theoretically harder to resist comprehensive warranties, indemnities and disclosure. This is because you, as the owner, retain ultimate responsibility for the performance of your team, including management. In this context, the manager is wearing two hats, one being the 'employed manager', the other being the 'third-party buyer'. From the manager's perspective, there is a clear conflict of interest, as they may know things that you do not, and for which they want warranty cover!

As a practical matter, it is common for warranties and indemnities to be somewhat 'watered-down' in the context of a sale to management, as everyone realises this conflict of interest, and management must ultimately accept some reasonability for their role and consequential level of knowledge.

Case Study

Mal has narrowed his options down to two potential sale transactions. The first being the roll-up transaction proposed by James, and the other being a straight sale to the national logistics company.

Mal's preferred transaction is the roll-up of the complimentary businesses of Ken and Alex, and then a sell-down of equity to a management team consisting of James and Ken.

The roll-up and sell-down transaction will be partly funded by an investment syndicate led by James' friend Edward. Mal will provide a level of vendor finance to the deal, as well as retain some equity.

The difficulty with the roll-up and sell-down transaction is that it consists of a combination of a 'related-party' manager, and two genuine arm's length parties (Edward and Ken). The arm's length parties will be looking for comprehensive warranties and indemnities to protect their interests, while Mal will be relying on James to assist him put together the disclosures, particularly about areas of the business over which James has day-to-day oversight. This is a common conflict of interest that arises in private equity backed management buyouts.

If Mal proceeds with the management team, Mal proposes to mitigate these risks by providing very broad disclosures and extensive material in the Data Room. He will then limit access to James and Edward. Ken will not be allowed into the Data Room until Mal has a legally binding contract that locks Ken into the transaction.

In essence, Mal will be saying to James and Edward: 'You don't need broad warranties and indemnities because I am giving you the full opportunity to make your own enquires about the business to assess the risks and opportunities for yourself.' In the context of a management buy-out, the risk of disclosing sensitive information to a current or future competitor in the Data Room is absent, because the management team already has broad access. Edward, as a financier, is not a competitor and is unlikely to become one.

In the short term, before a legally binding transaction is in place, Ken will need to rely on James and Edward to undertake the initial due diligence enquiries.

When a contract is in place, Mal can also give permission to James to disclose to the other members of the buy-out team anything James knows about the business, and then place a general limitation on the warranties and indemnities being anything that James knows, or ought reasonably to have known, because of his role in the business. This then places the onus on James to ensure that his team is aware of any skeletons.

As you can see, you need to carefully manage the interplay between the giving of warranties and indemnities, the level of due diligence allowed, and the level of disclosures.

Conditional Binding Offers

At this stage, all the competitive tension in the process should be resulting in Indicative Prices that meet (or exceed) your expectations. You should ask the remaining bidders to update their Indicative Prices following their initial due diligence enquiries, so you can assess who is still serious and whether any deal-breakers have been discovered during due diligence. If there is more than one bidder still in the process, then it is not unheard of for a bidder to raise their price following due diligence, because they have been able to satisfy themselves that a previously perceived risk is not material.

Hopefully, you still have more than one interested party to choose from. If this is the case, you have a choice to **go exclusive** with one of the bidders, or to try and continue to negotiate with more than one party.

You should have a fair idea of what a deal is going to look like with each party, including their price range and key terms. If the favoured bidder simply will not continue without exclusivity (which is probably going to be the case), then you may need to grant the exclusivity and move forward with one party.

At this stage you may still be **withholding sensitive commercial information**, and you certainly should not have allowed any of the bidders to meet key staff, suppliers or customers. Of course, they will have been pushing for this access for some time now…

You are likely to have reached a **chicken-and-egg impasse**. You do not want to disclose further information or disrupt your business operations before you have a deal legally locked-in, and the bidder will not legally commit to a purchase until they are satisfied about the content of the sensitive information, the attitude of key staff and third parties, and other commercial pre-conditions.

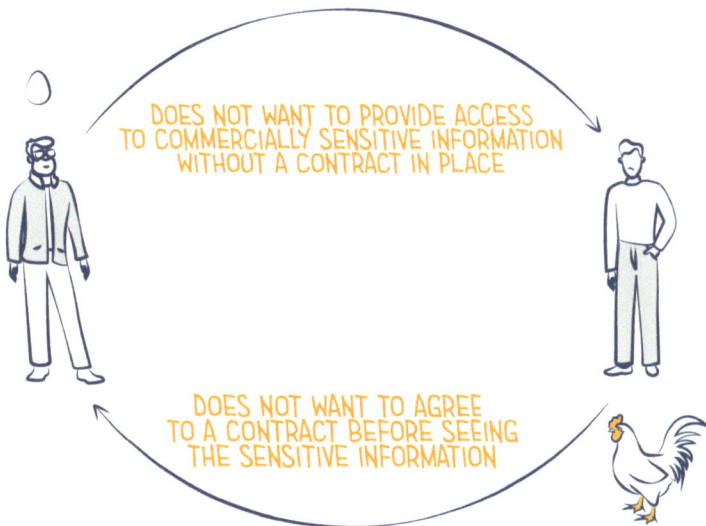

DOES NOT WANT TO PROVIDE ACCESS TO COMMERCIALLY SENSITIVE INFORMATION WITHOUT A CONTRACT IN PLACE

DOES NOT WANT TO AGREE TO A CONTRACT BEFORE SEEING THE SENSITIVE INFORMATION

This situation can be handled using a **Conditional Sale Contract**.

A Conditional Sale Contract is a legally binding document whereby you are bound to sell, and the bidder is bound to buy, *provided certain conditions are met*. Ideally the only difference between a final 'Sale Contract' and a Conditional Sale Contract, are the conditions relating to satisfactory *final* due diligence. For a relatively simple business, you can push for bidders to enter a Conditional Sale Contract even prior to *initial* due diligence.

The conditions in a Conditional Sale Contract relating to a second stage of final due diligence may include:

- ☑ Sensitive information meeting **objective criteria**. Most sensitive information is not actually deal-relevant, in that it is hard to come up with criteria whereby sensitive information can fail a pre-condition. For example, you may state in due diligence that no customer accounts for more than 10% of total revenue – but the sensitive information as to *who* your customers are really makes no difference. The same applies to confidential processes.

- ☑ Key suppliers and customers agreeing to **continue their dealings with the business post sale**. This may involve face-to-face meetings between these third parties and the buyer. This should never be allowed to occur without your presence, or the presence of one of your advisers.

- ☑ Identified **key employees agreeing to stay with the business** for a period and on identified terms. Once again, this may involve face-to-face meetings between the third parties and the buyer, with you present.

A buyer may request that the conditions are worded broadly, along the lines of 'concluding due diligence satisfactory to the buyer'. This is not really a due diligence condition, as it is completely up to the buyer to say if they are 'satisfied' or not. To draft an effective condition, the buyer needs to clearly specific what they need to see in their due diligence to be bound to purchase, in which case they can only walk away if those matters prove untrue.

A Conditional Sale Contract will also include other **conditions precedent** that are more mechanical in nature, and do not relate to sensitive information or key third parties. These include things like:

- ☑ The removal of **security interests** over business assets.

- ☑ The buyer **obtaining finance** of a certain amount to fund the purchase.

- ☑ Various **third parties providing their consent** to the change of control of the business, for example landlords, franchisors, key suppliers and customers.

- ☑ Various third parties agreeing to **assign or novate key business contracts**.

In summary, a conditional binding Sale Contract will enable you to lock in a legally binding deal *before*:

- Providing additional sensitive information to the buyer in a second stage of due diligence; and

- Providing access to third parties, such as key staff, suppliers, and customers.

The conditions imposed in the Sale Contract (by the prospective buyer) will help you in your 'buyer selection' process and protect the buyer if something adverse is discovered during the final stage of due diligence around sensitive information.

Of course, if your business does not involve any particularly sensitive information, and you are prepared to provide a bidder with unrestricted access prior to a legally binding deal, then you can fully negotiate the Sale Contract after you have selected the preferred bidder and they have completed their due diligence.

Case Study

When selecting between the management buy-out team and the third-party buyer, Mal elects to go exclusive with the management team because he can provide them with unrestricted access to the due diligence material without having to first negotiate a conditional Sale Contract.

Negotiating the Sale Contract

Experienced sellers and advisers appreciate that by the time the parties come to negotiate the Sale Contract (including a Conditional Sale Contract), most key 'commercial points' should have been addressed or negotiated between the buyer and seller, through disclosures in the Data Room and the Disclosure Letter, and through meetings with key staff.

Negotiations at this stage should be limited to alleviating prospective buyer concerns or issues – not reducing the up-front price.

There are many ways you can help alleviate or address prospective buyer concerns or fears without having to resort to a price reduction, including:

- Providing **additional due diligence** material;

- Offering **additional warranties**;

- Offering **specific indemnities**;

- Offering **vendor finance**;

- Providing or strengthening a **restraint of trade**;

- Agreeing to **provide training** where needed;

- Agreeing to **stay on as a consultant** to facilitate a smooth transition; and

- Offering 'claw-backs' and *future* **price adjustments** that are dependent on possible adverse events occurring, rather than a reduced up-front price in contemplation of such possibilities.

From a seller's perspective, if a buyer has stuck with you this far through the process, their inclination to walk-away based on not being able to re-negotiate price at the last minute is very low, but many will try this on.

From the buyer's perspective, this is a good time to ask for additional **contractual protections** that make sure you ultimately **get what you are paying for**. These will often be more valuable than a token drop in price. It will also preserve (and enhance) your relationships with the seller, which can prove very valuable in the future.

Documenting exactly what are you selling?

A Sale Contract for an <u>**Asset**</u> **Sale** is very different from the contract used for an <u>**Entity**</u> **Sale**. Most brokers do not fully appreciate the differences, and quite often the contracts prepared by brokers and accountants represent a confused mess between the two deal structures.

Another consideration to keep in mind is that a real estate agent may be licenced to sell a 'business' but they will not be licenced or qualified to sell 'shares' in a company. This requires an Australian Financial Services Licence (**AFSL**) from the Australian Securities and Investments Commission (**ASIC**). Once again, many brokers do not appreciate this fact. A real estate agent will not be covered by insurance in the context of a share transaction.

In short, make sure you have adopted the **best deal structure**, and then make sure you have the **appropriate documentation** for the type of deal you are doing.

Case Study

Mal has taken advice on the likely tax outcomes for him from either an **Asset Sale** or **share sale**. He is likely to do much better after-tax from a share sale. He understands that a share sale can be more complex to structure and document, but feels this is more than offset by the tax savings.

The ability to do a share sale is also helped by the fact that the management buy-out team are familiar with the company's history and know that Mal has kept things in his company relatively 'clean' over the years.

The management team has also set up an 'acquisition company' to be the legal entity that acquires:

- The shares in Mal's companies;
- The shares in Ken's company; and
- The assets of Alex's business.

At some point in the future, the management team may elect to liquidate the old companies and move all the business assets into 'clean' entities within the new group.

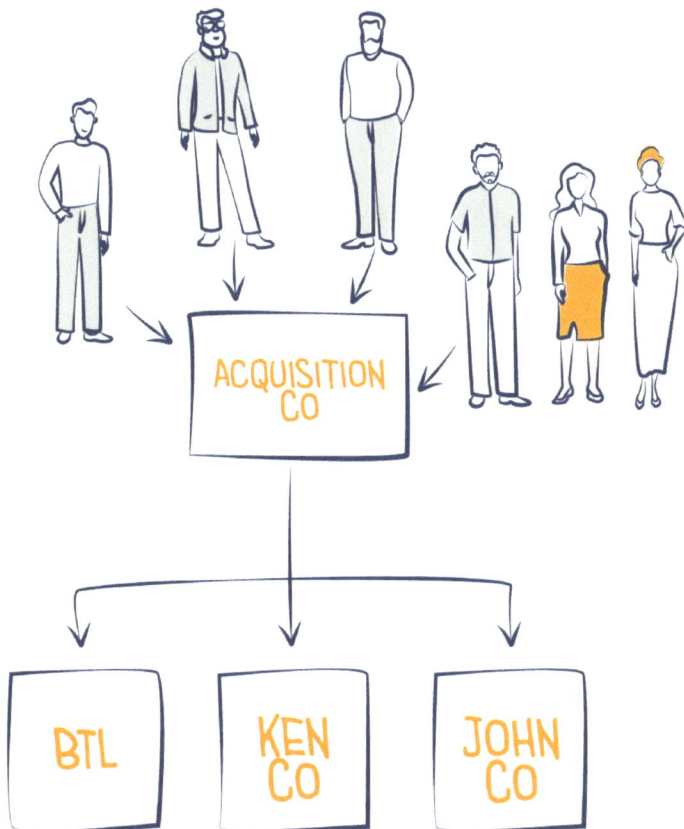

Key terms in an Asset Sale contract

The document used in the case of an Asset Sale is usually called a '**Business Sale Agreement**'. Several institutions have 'standard contracts' for this type of deal, including real estate institutes, law societies and conveyancing bodies. These templates have been 'designed by committee' and are not always clear and comprehensive.

An agreement for an **Asset Sale** is usually simpler than for an Entity Sale. This is because the buyer **only gets what the contract states**. If the contract says the buyer gets the tangible assets free of encumbrances and takes a transfer of several identified employees – that is all they get. Nothing more, or less. The buyer does not need to deal with the liabilities associated with trading that has taken place prior to settlement because they are not taking over the legal structure in which that trading occurred.

From the seller's perspective, they are only responsible to deliver what they promise in the contract. They are then left with the legal entity and any residual assets and liabilities.

The key terms you will see in a Business Sale Agreement are:

- ☑ What **assets** are being sold, (and you may also list specific assets that are not being sold).

- ☑ What **liabilities** are being assumed (if any). For example, equipment may be encumbered by third-party finance. Transferred employees will usually bring with them accrued entitlements.

- ☑ The **price** to be paid, including the agreed GST treatment. Many business sales will qualify for GST-free treatment as a *going concern*, but you should not just assume this to be the case.

- ☑ How the price will be **adjusted** at settlement. A few of the more common adjustments are for pre- and post-settlement revenue and expenses, pre-payments, deferred expenses and employee entitlements.

- ☑ How **employees** are to be treated, i.e. how the buyer will take over the transferring employees, and who is responsible for any staying behind.

- ☑ Any **pre-conditions** to settlement. For example, the release of security interests encumbering assets, consents to assignments and transfers of key contracts and the obtaining of finance.

- ☑ The mechanical processes whereby settlement will take place. For an Asset Sale, these processes can be quite detailed and prescriptive.

- ☑ A limited set of **warranties** and **indemnities**. Because the legal entity is remaining with the seller, there will be fewer required warranties and indemnities.

☑ Arrangement for accessing books and records, including who will keep the originals and who will have copies or access.

☑ What **assistance** the seller will provide post-settlement.

☑ Any **restraint of trade** on the seller (and their associates).

☑ Any **claw-back** or **earn-out** adjustments to the purchase price relating to the trading performance of the business post settlement.

☑ Any **related agreements** that need to be entered. For example, land sale contracts, contract assignments/ novations and employment contracts.

☑ Several schedules with lists and details of key deal elements.

Key terms in Entity Sale contract

The document used in an Entity Sale is usually called something like a '**Share Purchase Agreement**' (**SPA**), or in rarer instances, a 'Unit Sale Agreement'.

As already noted, an Entity Sale is a whole magnitude more complex than an Asset Sale from a **deal structure** perspective. However, this may not be immediately obvious. The sale transaction itself is very simple – usually the transfer of all the shares in the company from the seller to the buyer. The complexity arises because you are selling the **'net' value** in the entity at the time of settlement, and this net value is changing on an hour-to-hour basis as the business trades up to settlement.

The key terms of an agreement for an Entity Sale are:

☑ The agreement to **sell and buy the ownership interests** in the entity, usually the shares.

☑ Any **pre-conditions to settlement**, such as obtaining finance, approval of financial assistance, release of guarantees, and consents to the change of control under key contracts.

☑ A relatively simple **mechanism to achieve settlement**, because only the shares are being transferred. However, meetings may need to be held to remove and appoint directors, and to transfer control of banking arrangements.

☑ The preparation of **settlement or completion accounts** by a given date following completion, and a mechanism to **adjust the price** for any variation in the net equity of the entity disclosed by those accounts.

☑ **Comprehensive warranties and indemnities** about the entity being sold and its underlying assets and liabilities.

☑ A **separate taxation indemnity**. This is because the buyer will be taking on the historical tax position of the entity up to settlement.

☑ Any **restraint of trade** on the seller (and their associates).

☑ Any **claw-back** or **earn-out** adjustments to the purchase price relating to the trading performance of the business post settlement.

☑ Any **related agreements** that will need to be entered. For example, if the entity is using assets or property that are not owned by the entity being sold.

☑ Several schedules with lists and details of key deal elements.

The subtle art of drafting legal documents

There are many subtle drafting techniques that can radically change the risk profile of a deal for either the seller or buyer. Unless you have a lot of experience drafting these contracts you may not appreciate what these are.

A good example is how 'assets' are defined. If you are acting for the buyer, you should define plant and equipment as:

> *'all of the plant and equipment used in
> the usual course of the business, including
> those items listed in Schedule X'*

This will ensure you get *all* the assets used in the business, even if they are not listed, and even if they are currently subject to a lease or other encumbrance.

Whereas if you are acting for the seller, you would define plant and equipment as:

> *'all of the plant and equipment owned by
> the seller and listed in Schedule X'*

In this version the seller is only obliged to deliver the *listed items* and could legitimately remove any other items from the premises prior to settlement, even if they were being used in the business (although this may give rise to a breach of warranty). It also gives the seller a potential 'out' should one of the listed items end up not actually being *owned by the seller*.

Almost every clause and schedule item in a Sale Contract can be worded to either favour the seller or buyer, and even an experienced lawyer may not pick them all up, particularly if they do not work in this area regularly.

Dealing with employees

When selling your business, you will probably negotiate hard on things like the price, the assets being sold, and the settlement and handover period. What you may overlook is what will happen to your employees, and what this might cost you down the track. This can be a serious mistake, impacting not only your hip pocket, but the effective transition of your business into new hands.

The main thing to keep in mind with employees is that their **entitlements** attach to **whoever employs them**.

In the case of an **Entity Sale**, the employer will be the entity that conducts the business, both before and after settlement. If you have agreed to sell the entity, the employees (and their entitlements) will **automatically go to the buyer** with the entity. The buyer will inherit all of the employees by virtue of the change in underlying ownership of the entity, and will thereafter be responsible for their entitlements – whether they accrued before or after the settlement.

However, if the sale is structured as an **Asset Sale**, the buyer may leave behind some or all of the employees. Unless some positive action is taken, you as the seller will retain both the employees and the responsibility for their entitlements. This is where things can get tricky.

Dealing with employees in an Asset Sale

If the assets of your business are being sold (rather than the business entity), the buyer has three options when dealing with **each** employee. The buyer can:

- Not offer them employment;

- Offer them employment, but without recognition of their prior service. (Note that this option is not available to a buyer who is associated with the seller); or

- Offer them employment, and with recognition of their prior service.

There are different outcomes for you as the seller depending on what option the buyer selects, (or is required to select under the Sale Contract). Also bear in mind that the buyer may use a combination of the above options among your staff, as the buyer may wish to transfer some employees, and not others.

The employee outcomes – both financial and logistical – for you as the seller must be considered and negotiated into the Sale Contract, or you may end up with less than you bargained for.

Option 1: No offer of employment

If a buyer decides not to offer an employee new employment, the employee will remain with their original employer, i.e. you. However, once the business is sold, the employee's role is likely to become **redundant**, as there is no business for the employee to work in. This means that the employee will be terminated by way of redundancy on the completion of the business sale.

This termination triggers **all the ordinary entitlements** that an employee has in cases of genuine redundancy. You will be required to pay out all their entitlements, both at law and under their employment contract, including accrued annual leave, termination notice pay, redundancy pay and any *pro-rata* long service leave entitlements (if they have vested).

Terminating employees due to a business sale can potentially be an expensive outcome for you as the seller. Accordingly, you need to budget for these employee terminations in negotiating your business sale terms (including the purchase price) and in allocating your sale proceeds.

Option 2: Employment without recognition of prior service

A buyer who is dealing with you at arm's length (i.e. not a related party) can choose not to recognise an employee's prior service with you as the seller. This means the buyer can elect to offer your employees employment with their purchasing entity, but without recognising continuity of service for certain purposes.

In this scenario, you are deemed to have terminated the employee at settlement, and thereafter the employee commences **new employment** with the buyer. This can be an attractive proposition for the buyer, as they get the benefit of an employee who has experience and proven performance in the business, while having the upside of resetting the clock in terms of certain employee entitlements and the 'minimum employment period' (i.e. probation).

You as the seller must **pay out all the employee's accrued entitlements on settlement**. You must also provide termination notice (or pay in lieu) and redundancy pay to the employee, as the transfer of the business has affected their job by severing their continuity of service. Redundancy pay is only required to be paid if you would ordinarily be required to pay it. If you qualify as a 'small business employer' redundancy pay is not applicable.

While the buyer gets to press reset on some things, they must still recognise accrued entitlements relating to personal/carer's leave and parental leave, and the right to request flexible working arrangements. Any service a transferring employee had with the you as seller will count as service with the buyer for these purposes. This may require some adjustment between the parties as part of the business sale because the buyer is required to assume liability for these entitlements which the employee may use in the future.

Similarly, most state legislation relating to **long service leave** will provide that the employee's service with the seller carries over to the buyer (as the new employer) for the purposes of calculating long service leave entitlements. If you pay out accrued pro-rated long service leave entitlements to the employee at completion, it does not 'stop the clock' but instead gets counted towards their total entitlement. When the employee serves long enough with their new employer (the buyer), and their total service length qualifies them for long service leave, they are entitled to receive the difference between their entitlement at law and what they have already been paid by their old employer (being you the seller). Again, there may need to be some adjustment between the parties to account for this.

If this option is adopted, the terms and conditions of the employee's employment with the buyer will still be covered by any 'transferable instrument', which is any enterprise agreement, workplace determination, other registered agreement or award that applied to their employment with you as the seller. This means that the employee's overarching terms and conditions of employment are protected, despite the transfer of the business.

This option is often preferred by parties to a transaction, because it clearly denotes the end of one employment relationship and the beginning of another. However, the disadvantage for the seller is that it triggers an obligation to pay entitlements that would not otherwise have yet arisen.

Option 3: Employment with recognition of prior service

This option is the most common method adopted by parties to a business sale. This is likely because of a lack of clear understanding about the other options.

Under this option, the employees of the business suffer minimum interruption to their employment terms. The buyer may prefer this option because:

- It may result in a lower purchase price (as adjusted for the entitlements);

- The employees can take planned leave shortly after settlement without going into a leave deficit; and

- This method gets the employment relationship with the buyer off on the right foot.

If the buyer offers ongoing employment with recognition of prior service to the employee, what they are effectively offering is that they will take up where the seller left off. This means they become responsible for all the accrued entitlements of the employee that have not been taken or paid out to date. Because of this, the buyer will want some compensation from the seller for assuming the employee entitlement liabilities. The question then arises: what adjustment should be made to compensate the buyer?

There are myriad approaches that can be adopted for adjusting employee entitlements, and there is not right or wrong way – it is a matter of what can be negotiated. As the seller, you will want to limit the adjustment as much as possible. On the other hand, the buyer will be looking to maximise the adjustment, to be compensated upfront for the future use of the accrued entitlements by employees.

Commonly, the actual accrued entitlements up to the date of completion are adjusted either in full, or at a lower 'tax-adjusted' value. These entitlements are valued as if the employee was terminated on settlement. This includes accrued and unpaid wages/salary, leave entitlements and superannuation guarantee amounts.

This just leaves the question of how to deal with personal/carer's leave entitlements and long service leave entitlements. These entitlements are more difficult to adjust, because the employee may never access these entitlements. If they are adjusted, the buyer may get a windfall, depending on what happens in the future. On the other hand, if the parties adjust for less than the full value of these entitlements, the seller may get a windfall if all the entitlements are taken.

Obviously, the preference for you as the seller would be to make no adjustment at all and leave these entitlements as a cost for the buyer to assume. You may be surprised by what the buyer is willing to take on in this regard – many buyers see these potential entitlements as a business purchase expense, and part of the cost of 'buying' loyal, long-standing employees.

If these 'uncertain' entitlements are to be adjusted, the parties will often negotiate a fixed percentage adjustment – somewhere between 20% and 70% – of the monetary value of the accrued personal/carer's leave entitlement and long service leave entitlement as at completion.

Very rarely, particularly in some larger transactions, the seller and buyer may agree that the buyer will take responsibility for the primary obligation, and seek reimbursement from the seller *as and when* the accrued leave is taken after settlement by way of a **specific indemnity**. Of course, this relies on the seller being around and having the capacity to reimburse for a period following settlement.

What if an employee does not accept employment?

An issue that can arise – and has been the subject of several court decisions – is what happens if the buyer makes an offer of employment to an existing employee, which is rejected by the employee?

Provided the employment offer is on terms and conditions similar (and no less favourable) to their current employment terms, and recognises continuity of service, an employee who does not accept the offer will **not be entitled to redundancy pay**. However, the employee will still be entitled to receive payment of their accrued entitlements and payment for any termination notice period from their existing employer (being you, the seller).

Transferring employee records

Under the *Fair Work Regulations*, the seller must provide the buyer with the employee record relating to each transferring employee at settlement. If the transferring employee becomes an employee of the buyer post completion, the buyer must ask the seller to provide a copy of the employee record concerning the transferring employee.

The buyer must then keep the employee records as if they had been made by the buyer at the time at which they were made by the seller (as the old employer), which means that they must be stored for at least 7 years.

Dealing proactively with your employees

Early discussions with the buyer about how they wish to deal with employees, and who will look after the employee entitlements, can save you time and money (and headaches) in the long run. At a minimum, you should ensure that you leave sufficient time to give employees termination notice, and for the buyer to negotiate employment offers with transferring employees. The earlier the issue is put on the table, the stronger your position is to negotiate a favourable outcome for you and your employees.

Conditions precedent

Even after a definitive Sale Contract has been signed by all parties, the deal is not yet done. Conditions precedent are the conditions that must be satisfied (or waived) before the parties are obligated to complete or 'settle' the transaction. If one or more of these conditions cannot be satisfied, then one or other party will have the option to either 'waive' the condition and proceed to settle, or terminate the contract and walk away.

As noted above, in a Conditional Sale Contract, one of the key conditions may be the buyer undertaking and being satisfied with a second stage of due diligence about sensitive financial and operational matters.

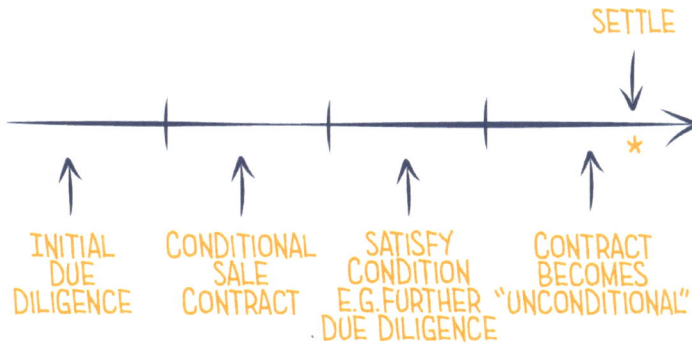

SETTLE

INITIAL DUE DILIGENCE

CONDITIONAL SALE CONTRACT

SATISFY CONDITION E.G. FURTHER DUE DILIGENCE

CONTRACT BECOMES "UNCONDITIONAL"

Who benefits from conditions precedent?

Conditions precedent are usually for the **benefit of the buyer**. This means that if the condition is not satisfied, the buyer can elect to waive the condition and move forward, or walk away from the deal.

However, conditions precedent can also be for the benefit of the seller. Ordinarily, if the seller is not able to deliver what they promise under the Sale Contract, the buyer can sue for damages or specific performance. So, if the seller is concerned that they may not be able to deliver, say, a consent from a landlord, they can make the obtaining of this consent a 'seller condition precedent'. If the condition cannot be satisfied, then the seller can cancel the sale without penalty. (Such a condition may also be a buyer condition precedent, that is, the condition is for the benefit of *both* the seller and the buyer.)

What sort of things are covered by conditions precedent?

Typical buyer conditions precedent, (i.e. conditions that give the buyer an out), include:

- ☑ Completing **due diligence** of sensitive financial and operational matters.

- ☑ Getting **sufficient finance** to fund the purchase on acceptable commercial terms.

- ☑ Obtaining any **statutory or regulatory licences, consents or approvals** (e.g. from FIRB in the case of a foreign buyer).

- ☑ Having executed agreements in place with **key employees**, **key suppliers**, and **key customers**.

- ☑ **Discharging debts / security interests** over the business assets.

- ☑ Real property **lease assignments or consents**.

- ☑ Tax clearances.

Typical seller conditions precedent, (i.e. conditions that give the seller an out), include:

- ☑ Obtaining any **consents to assignment or novation** of assets, contracts and leases.

- ☑ **Release of guarantees** given by the seller directors to suppliers.

It is customary to include a provision that requires the parties to use all reasonable, commercial endeavours to satisfy the conditions precedent. Otherwise, the conditions can turn the Sale Contract into an 'option' for the party benefitting from the condition, rather than a binding deal.

The seller needs to be careful to negotiate conditions that are very clear as to what needs to be satisfied, and what the relevant parties need to do to satisfy the condition. The conditions should also have very clear end-dates by which they need to be satisfied.

Case Study

The management team want to include a very widely drafted condition precedent that they can raise a certain amount of equity from Edward's syndicate to fund the cash element of the deal on terms agreeable to them within 60 days of signing the Share Sale Contract.

This essentially turns the Share Sale Contract into an 'option' for them to purchase the business lasting for up to 60 days.

While Mal is prepared to accept such an open-ended condition, he needs to accept that he has not really 'concluded' a deal with the team until the end of the 60 days. He must resist providing the buyer with significant access to his business during this period and until the contract becomes unconditional.

Opt-in versus opt-out conditions

From a seller's perspective, conditions are best drafted as *opt-out*, rather than *opt-in*.

For example, an *opt-in* finance condition would be worded as:

> *'The contract is conditional on the buyer
> notifying the seller, before 30 June, that the
> buyer has obtained satisfactory finance'*

If the buyer does nothing, the contract will terminate if notice has *not* been given by the buyer to the seller by 30 June.

Whereas an *opt-out* version of the same condition would be drafted to say:

> *'The contract is conditional on the buyer
> notifying the seller, before 30 June, that it
> has <u>not</u> obtained satisfactory finance'*

Under the opt-out version, the contract will automatically become unconditional on 30 June unless the buyer **takes the positive step** of telling the seller they have not been able to get finance.

Settlement (or completion)

When the Sale Contract has been signed, and the conditions precedent satisfied or waived, the parties' focus then turns to the mechanics of payment and hand-over. This process is usually referred to as '**settlement**' in Asset Sales, and '**completion**' in Entity Sales. Both terms mean the same thing.

Settlement can be a very busy time for everyone involved in the transaction. You should use a **Settlement Checklist** to ensure that no administrative or procedural matters are overlooked.

The Sale Contract and the Settlement Checklist should cover all the mechanical aspects of settlement, including timing, location, format, and the procedures. This will avoid any last-minute confusion or unnecessary surprises. For larger deals, it is common for the professional advisers to have a trial-run of settlement a week or so prior to the actual date.

Dealing with the money

In most cases the buyer will need to deliver an agreed amount of cleared funds on or before settlement. If the seller is providing an amount of vendor finance, the buyer will need to formally acknowledge this debt back to the seller at settlement.

It is common for the buyer to deposit the required cash into their lawyer's trust account prior to settlement, and for the lawyer to then disburse the funds to the seller's solicitor's trust account on the settlement day. This enables both sides to independently verify that the payment obligation has been met and received.

Use of escrow arrangements and solicitor undertakings

Even with the best of plans, things can go wrong at settlement. To keep things moving and on track, the lawyers acting for both parties may agree to hold certain signed documents in 'escrow' and/or provide 'solicitor undertakings' on behalf of their respective clients. The effect of this is to place elements of the deal in "no man's land" for a short period while these administrative things get sorted out, while not holding up the rest of the settlement processes.

When this occurs, the solicitors on both sides are professionally (and legally) obliged to act in an unbiased way to ensure that the suspended matters are sorted out, as agreed. Before agreeing to do this, your lawyer will ask for your written instructions to underpin their undertakings.

Conditions subsequent

From a practical perspective, by the time settlement occurs, only half of the real work has been completed. In the case of an Asset Sale, it may take many months to obtain all the necessary **consents** and attend to the **registration** of changes of ownership of assets on public registers. This post-settlement work is often underestimated by all parties.

Unfortunately, in many cases, this work just does not get done. It may only be discovered years down the track that ownership of a registered trademark was not transferred with IP Australia, or a lease assignment was not registered against the property title, or a personal guarantee for a trade account was not lifted.

Whether you are buying or selling, you need to make a **comprehensive list** of what needs to be attended to *post*-settlement, and make sure you have **clearly allocated responsibility** to ensure these tasks are done.

Preparation of completion accounts

If the transaction was structured as an **Entity Sale**, then a key *condition subsequent* will be preparing the **completion accounts**, and the payment of any **post-completion adjustments**.

The completion accounts are a special-purpose set of financial accounts used to calculate the '**net value**' of the entity that has been sold on the **day of completion**. This net value is then compared with an agreed net enterprise value adopted in the Share Purchase Agreement,[13] and any positive or negative difference is paid to or by the seller.

The completion accounts are basically a special purpose Balance Sheet, but in order to get this right, revenue and expenses up to completion will need to be calculated, so in effect, they are a full set of accounts with the object of producing one key number – the **completion day net asset position**.

To prepare the completion accounts, the parties need to know all the transactions that have occurred between the last set of formal accounts (on which the settlement day price estimate is likely to have been calculated) up to the completion date. The full details of these transactions are unlikely to be known until a period following completion, so the completion accounts are generally prepared within a period of 30 to 90 days following completion (depending on the sophistication of the entity's accounting system and the nature of the business).

The Share Purchase Agreement must include a detailed mechanism for preparing, reviewing and verifying the completion accounts, and resolving any disputes. When this mechanism has been properly applied, any **post-completion adjustment payment** is then made. An adjustment payment can go either way, depending on whether the completion day net asset position is above or below the projected value used in the Share Purchase Agreement.

You may think it is easy to identify the transactions leading up to completion, and their impact on net value, but accounting is never that simple. When is revenue recognised? When does an expense or liability arise? There is plenty of room for debate.

One critical factor is ensuring that the **basis** or **methodology** used to estimate the net assets prior to completion, and the basis or methodology used to calculate the completion accounts net assets, are the same. Often the estimated value is simply adopted from the entity's management accounts, whereas the Share Purchase Agreement may require the application of standard accounting principles (such as Australian or international accounting standards) to determine net assets in the completion accounts. This can result in massive variations from what is expected.[14]

Even after taking all these precautions, there is still likely to be some argument at the last minute over the completion account adjustment.

Completion Accounts Method

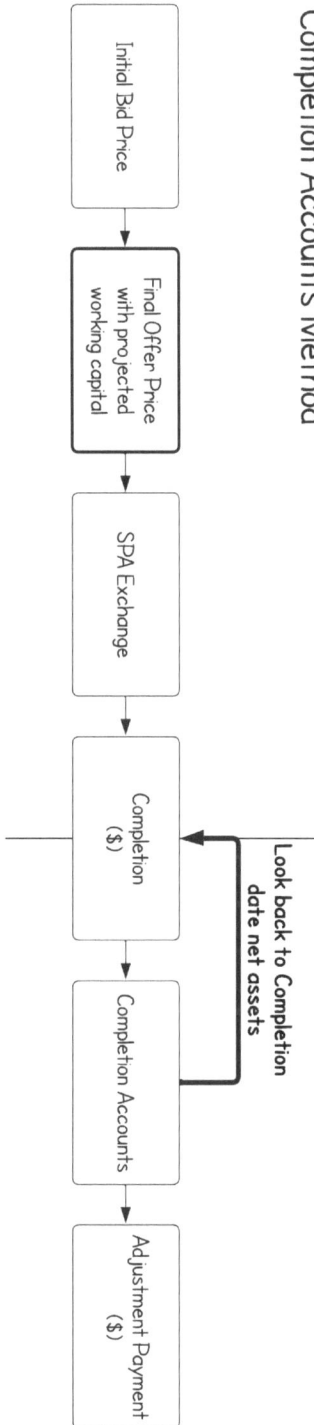

```
┌─────────────────┐      ┌──────────────────┐      ┌─────────────────┐
│                 │      │   Final Offer    │      │                 │
│ Initial Bid     │ ───► │   Price          │ ───► │  SPA Exchange   │
│ Price           │      │   with projected │      │                 │
│                 │      │   working capital│      │                 │
└─────────────────┘      └──────────────────┘      └─────────────────┘
```

Completion ($) ◄── Look back to Completion date net assets ── Completion Accounts ──► Adjustment Payment ($)

The 'locked-box' alternative

The completion account mechanism means that the risk and benefits of trading up to completion remains with the seller, and the buyer does not know the final price they will need to pay until a period after completion.

In our view, the completion accounts mechanism is the most robust, and there is little downside for either party. If the net value of the business under the completion accounts is significantly higher than the estimated enterprise value in the Share Purchase Agreement, the buyer will have the benefit of that additional value to fund the price adjustment.

However, to avoid the price 'uncertainty' associated with completion accounts, some parties elect to adopt a 'locked-box' completion mechanism. Under this scenario, the parties agree to a date prior to signing the Share Purchase Agreement on which the enterprise value and sale value will be struck (the '**locked-box date**'). The **buyer** then has the benefit (and risk) of trading from the locked-box date. The seller agrees not to move any value out of the entity from the locked-box date in the Share Purchase Agreement, (i.e. to avoid 'leakage' other than what may be agreed with the buyer).

This mechanism can simplify the *post*-completion tasks. The parties will no doubt attempt to 'estimate' the benefit of trading from the locked-box date to completion and reflect this estimate in their fixed negotiated price.

The locked-box approach is particularly suited to transactions where the parties require certainty (e.g. private equity exits) rapid integration of the business into the buyer's operations is necessary, or as a way of reducing risks associated with buyers trying to bridge a value gap through completion accounts adjustments (i.e. 'price-chipping').

Locked-box Method

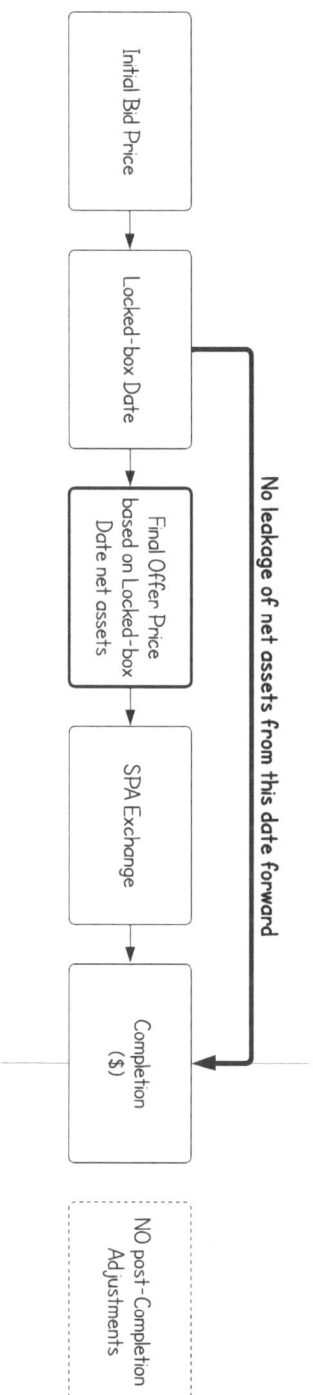

```
┌──────────────┐      ┌──────────────┐      ┌──────────────────┐      ┌──────────────┐      ┌──────────────┐
│              │      │              │      │  Final Offer     │      │              │      │              │
│  Initial Bid │ ───▶ │ Locked-box   │ ───▶ │  Price based on  │ ───▶ │ SPA Exchange │ ───▶ │  Completion  │
│    Price     │      │    Date      │      │  Locked-box      │      │              │      │     ($)      │
│              │      │              │      │  Date net assets │      │              │      │              │
└──────────────┘      └──────┬───────┘      └──────────────────┘      └──────────────┘      └──────┬───────┘
                             │                                                                      ▲
                             └──────────────────────────────────────────────────────────────────────┘
                              No leakage of net assets from this date forward
```

┌ ─ ─ ─ ─ ─ ─ ─ ─ ┐
  NO post-Completion
  Adjustments
└ ─ ─ ─ ─ ─ ─ ─ ─ ┘

Mal and the management team agree to adopt a traditional 'completion accounts' mechanism and adjust the sale price within 45 days after completion.

The most recent management accounts prepared a little over a month prior to completion indicate a 'net equity' value of $8.2 million. This is the price that is adopted in the Share Purchase Agreement and paid on completion.

When the completion accounts are prepared a month or so later, they disclose a net equity value of $8.8 million, which is $600,000 above the completion value. This becomes an additional amount payable by the management team to Mal.

Deferred consideration and withholdings

A savvy buyer may request that a portion of the purchase price be held back, pending satisfaction of certain conditions subsequent,[15] or as security against future potential warranty claims. It is common for these withheld amounts to be held by either the buyer or seller's lawyer in their trust account pending satisfaction of the contingencies.

It is critical that you agree on a clear mechanism for claims against the withheld amount to be properly made, assessed, disputed and ultimately rejected or paid.

Other price adjustments

The final purchase price paid by the buyer may be adjusted for other outcomes or contingencies not known at the time of execution of the Sale Contract. For example, a purchase price adjustment might be based on the results of a stocktake, a future sales result, whether all assignments have been satisfied, and 'earn-outs' and 'claw-backs' for certain events or results.

Earn-outs

Earn-outs are a special type of price adjustment that is based on the **future performance** of the business. These are quite common in transactions of all sizes.

Unfortunately, in many transactions where an earn-out is included, a dispute ultimately arises as to whether a payment is due, and for how much.

This largely arises from the difficulty of identifying what the earn-out will be based on. If it is based on a 'net' concept, like net margin or profit, then it is quite easy for the buyer to manipulate this through higher expenditure over the earn-out period. For this reason, it is preferable to base it on a 'gross' concept, like revenue. But this can also be manipulated, for example, if the buyer decreases turnover in favour of higher margins, defers revenue, or moves revenue to another entity.

If the buyer has other operations, it can be hard to identify the relevant metric within the context of the combined businesses following settlement. It is also easy for the buyer to move revenue or profits out of the 'business' that was purchased or move expenses into the business. Accordingly, the metrics used should be based on the performance of the buyer's overall business. However, this can sometimes disadvantage the seller if the buyer's original business was not as successful.

It is preferable to use earn-outs as **downside-protection for the buyer**, rather than upside for the seller. This means that the buyer should expect to pay the full earn-out if the business continues to perform satisfactorily after settlement. The earn-out would only abate if things turned unexpectedly negative.

The alternative is to use an earn-out as an **upside-incentivise to the seller** to stay involved in the business and to help it grow. These earn-outs inevitably lead to dispute, as the seller will believe that it was the buyer's actions that caused the business to underperform and abate the earn out.

Put simply, it's hard to design an effective earn-out that is not going to leave one or other party disappointed. You should aim to make any earn-out period relatively short, and put in place a mechanism for the payments to be objectively determined by a truly independent party on objective criteria.

Taking equity in the buyer

If you are selling to a buyer whose shares are listed on a public market, or to a private equity backed roll-up, then you may be offered 'shares' or 'equity' as part of the sale price, in lieu of cash.

Whether you accept this is ultimately an **investment decision**. You should ask yourself: '*If I received 100% cash for my business, would I turn around and invest a part of that cash in the buyer?*' If your answer is no, then you should either not accept the equity, or adjust your sale price up to 'discount' the cost of the equity to a point where you would choose to make the investment.

You need to be particularly careful with private equity backed buyers. These are often highly leveraged enterprises, and the true value of the equity you receive can swing widely. There will also be some period during which the equity will not be liquid, i.e. you will not be able to sell, so you need to be very sure you believe in the competency of the buying enterprise's management.

There are also potential tax consequences of taking equity in lieu of cash. Put simply, you are likely to be taxed on the 'gain' you make from selling your business, even if you receive the proceeds in illiquid equity rather than cash. You will not be able to pay your tax bill with equity, so you need to plan how you will fund this liability. (However, for transactions involving shares, there are potential tax 'roll-overs' to defer this tax liability to a later time when you sell the replacement interests. There are also tax concessions and roll-overs for qualifying small businesses.)

Case Study

Mal agrees to take shares in the management team's acquisition entity as part of the consideration he receives for selling his shares in BTL Pty Ltd and BTL Holdings.

The management team gives Mal an option to sell these shares back to the management team after 3 years at a value set with reference to the overall performance of the business.

Because Mal is selling BTL Pty Ltd and BTL Holdings as entities (i.e. he is selling his shares), Mal can defer paying tax up-front on the value of these replacement shares by applying the scrip-for-scrip rollover in the capital gains tax provisions.

Mal also agrees to provide a level of vendor finance to the management team. Mal will therefore swap some of the value of his shares in BTL Pty Ltd and BTL Holdings for a 'new asset' in the form of a 'loan' to the management team's acquisition entity. Mal will not be able to defer the tax liability on this portion of the sale price, and will therefore need to pay his tax liability out of the remaining cash element of the sale price.

Press release

As the seller, you are likely to be less concerned about how the sale is communicated to third parties. On the other hand, the buyer will want to place the best spin on the transaction, to maintain and maximise the value of what they have bought.

A plan for this post-settlement communication process should be incorporated into the Sale Contract. For example, you may wish to ensure the sale price is not publicly disclosed by the buyer. The buyer may wish for you to make statements that are consistent with their future strategies.

It is common for the seller and buyer to agree on one or more '**joint statements**' about the transaction. There may be an internal statement for employees, one for key third parties like suppliers and customers, and one for the public, including public investment markets. The idea is to plan for consistent (non-contradictory) statements from all parties.

Case Study

By carefully following a well-planned sale process, Mal has been able to:

- Roll-up his business with Ken and Alex's businesses, to form a larger and more competitive national logistics company;

- Pass day-to-day operational control and responsibility to the younger management team led by James and Ken;

- Take some cash off the table through the sale of a controlling stake in BTL Pty Ltd and BTL Holdings, funded by the investor syndicate brought to the deal by Edward;

- Swap some equity value into an income-producing asset in the form of vendor finance to the acquisition company;

- Retain some future 'value upside' through his ongoing shareholding in the management team's acquisition company;

- Retain the Sydney depot as a passive asset on which he derived a commercial rate of rent; and

- Overall, realise a fantastic value for his lifelong efforts in building BTL!

8

Important Strategic Issues

Maintaining a tight timeframe

If you want a fantastic deal, then you need three things:

☑ First, you need to have your business in **'deal-ready' shape** before you start the process. You do not want to be grasping around for information half-way through the deal process.

☑ Secondly, you need a **professional team** who is ready, right from the word go, to handle every element of the deal through to completion. They need to have all their checklists ready, all contracts ready, and enough resources to effectively execute the process. This material should not be put together along the way.

☑ Finally, you need to set a **clear agenda** to conclude the deal, and then stick to it like glue.

You need to be able to create and sustain **commercial pressure** on everyone involved in the deal, from start to finish. You need to start and remain 'ahead of the deal' as it unfolds. In this way, you will maintain control of all outcomes.

When to go exclusive

You may have gathered that **competitive tension** is hugely important in the sale process. The truth is, without real competitive tension **YOU WILL NOT SELL YOUR BUSINESS**. This is a proposition that is rarely proved wrong.

This does not mean you will fail to sell your business if there is only one interested party. It means that without a credible 'Plan-B' option, for example, keeping your business under professional management, you will not get that prospective buyer over the line.

If you have more than one interested party, then you should design a sale process that defers the point in time when you go exclusive with only one party. Furthermore, exclusivity should be conditional on the selected bidder meeting several closely spaced, periodic milestones. If the bidder fails to meet a milestone, then you should have the option to terminate the exclusivity and bring the other parties back into the deal.

The role of your lawyer

It is the role of your advisers to provide you with relevant **information** and **options**, including providing an insight into the likely commercial consequences of *your choices*.

However, it is not the role of your advisers to make commercial calls on your behalf.

While your lawyer will 'negotiate' many aspects of the Sale Contract, do not abdicate responsibility for deciding on the **commercial terms**. Most lawyers are not very good at making commercial judgements. They are good at documenting *what you tell them to document*.

For your lawyer, there is nothing more frustrating that dealing with an opposing lawyer who is taking it upon themselves to make commercial calls (usually bad ones), and often without their client's clear instructions. You can usually tell if your lawyer is overstepping the line if there is any animosity with their opposing counsel. The role of lawyers in a transaction should be to act as the calming oil in between the two commercial parties, and not as sandpaper.

You should instruct your lawyer to **bring any commercial points to you for your consideration**. Furthermore, your lawyer should recognise, with their opposing counsel, when a matter is truly commercial in nature, for the parties to decide, rather than something they should be debating. The lawyers should only ever debate **how best to document** what has already been decided between the parties.

If you adopt this approach, your legal bill will be significantly reduced, the deal is likely to proceed at a faster pace, and in a more amicable fashion.

Using a professional negotiator

If you do not like the process of negotiation, then engaging the services of a professional negotiator is a viable option. Many people think this is what they are getting when they engage their lawyer. But unfortunately, most lawyers have **no formal training in negotiation skills**, and have the wrong personality for it.

Even if you do find a person capable of negotiating on your behalf, you will still carry the responsibility for the **final commercial calls**. You simply cannot avoid this. Even if this does not come naturally to you, try to enjoy it!

9

Acquisition Strategy

Many of the strategies a prospective buyer should employ are, as logic would suggest, simply the opposite of what is recommend for a seller.

Rather than providing an exhaustive explanation of each step in the process from the buyer's perspective, set out below are selected key issues that you, as a buyer, should consider at various stages.

As you will have gathered from the advice to sellers, the party who maintains **effective control** over the sale process will ultimately control the outcomes. You can exert and maintain control through thorough **preparation** and relentless **execution**.

As the buyer, you need a clear strategy about how you will go about **selecting potential targets** and **executing transactions**. The more you do of these types of transactions, the better you will get at it. Be aware - it can become a bit addictive!

In this part we will refer to a case study involving the acquisition of a small specialist law firm by a more diversified and established law firm.

Case Study

Angela runs an established law firm that practices across several areas of law in two states, New South Wales and South Australia.

Angela wants to beef-up her operations in NSW and thinks that acquiring a small law firm will accelerate her progress towards this goal.

Let's join Angela through the acquisition process.

Buy what you know

As a buyer you should be actively looking for businesses that you know something about. Focus on businesses that operate in an industry, or with assets, that you have significant experience in or have thoroughly researched.

This is particularly so if you are looking for a bargain, or a distressed business you wish to turn around. The chances of you being able to run a business better than the previous owner are next to zero, unless you come to the business already knowing more about the industry than the previous owner.

If this is your first acquisition, there will be a lot of learning about the acquisition and merger **process** itself. You do not need the additional complexity of understanding a new industry.

Case Study

Angela has been running her own law firm for almost 20 years and has a good idea of how the 'business of law' works. Acquiring another practice and bolting it on to her existing practice clearly falls within the scope of her expertise and experience.

That said, although Angela has helped many of her clients buy and sell a business, this is the first time she is venturing into this area on her own behalf!

Angela has reviewed the information for several deals, but so far none have fallen within the sweet spot of size and opportunity. Most have been very small practices and centered around a single individual practitioner retiring from the law at an advanced age. Angela has not been able to justify any real value in this scenario because the practitioner and their clients have been at the tail-end of their business lives.

There have been a couple of larger opportunities. However, given the likely cost and scale, if anything went wrong with these opportunities, it would likely take Angela' business with them – a risk that Angela does not have an appetite for.

However, Angela has now come across what she considers to be the 'Goldilocks' scenario: an older practitioner, Tom, is looking to retire and pass on his 11-person legal practice.

Don't over-invest in the process

You must be disciplined (and unemotional) in your approach to potential acquisitions. Only buy and pay for **quality** and be prepared to move on if your enquires reveal that quality is not present.

You must manage your level of emotional engagement and financial investment in the purchase process. The best way to do this is to engage quality advisers who will have the confidence and experience to provide you unbiased and frank opinions. You must remain aware of the fact that ego and pride can lead you to acquire something with low potential, and at a price that cannot be justified.

Putting in place systems to ensure you remain calm, objective and rational will also assist in creating the perception you are not 'desperate' to get the deal done.

Case Study

Angela has engaged her friend Tim, who is an accountant, to be her 'rational self', to critically review any deals Angela comes across from an external and dispassionate perspective.

Tim has already helped Angela cool-off on several deals that just didn't add up.

Having reviewed the information about Tom's legal practice, Tim agrees with Angela that this opportunity is worth pursuing.

Secure exclusivity early

You must secure the right to deal exclusively with the seller as early as possible. This will reduce competitive tension, and thereby enable you to be more inquisitive during due diligence, and more aggressive in your contract negotiations. Early exclusivity will secure a better price and more favourable terms.

Ideally, you can avoid a competitive process entirely by **proactively approaching potential sellers** – before they have even seriously considered selling their business. We have worked with entrepreneurs who have based their entire growth strategy around making **unsolicited approaches** to potential businesses. They usually end up acquiring them for very reasonable prices in a simple and completely uncontested acquisition process.

Case Study

Tom flirted with selling his law firm to several parties prior to meeting Angela. Tom went down the sale path at least twice with senior lawyers working for him, and once with an external party.

Neither senior lawyer had the cash to fund a buyout. They also felt that Tom should effectively 'give' them the business, given how long they had worked for him.

Tom called-off the negotiations with the external party when they made it clear that Tom would need to exit the business as from settlement, i.e. they would instigate a 'clean break'. Tom is keen to ensure that his clients are looked after, and believes this will require his active involvement for a period of time after selling.

When Angela arrived on the scene, the landscape was relatively clear. By the time Angela and Tom started to really negotiate over the possible terms of a sale, Angela had been talking with Tom for over 6 months.

Angela did not require Tom to formally commit to exclusivity, as it was apparent that Angela was the last person standing. She was in a relatively good position to reach acceptable terms with Tom that would minimise her downside.

10

Structuring the Acquisition

Asset Purchase versus Entity Purchase

Generally, as a buyer you will prefer a 'cleaner' **Asset Purchase** and thereby avoid the issue of taking on the historical liabilities and encumbrances of the seller's legal 'entity'.

However, you should not rule out an **Entity Purchase**. Buying the entity may afford advantages in certain scenarios, including:

- ☑ If the business being acquired has many **contracts** and/or **licences** that can more easily be acquired as part of the legal entity. An Asset Purchase would require many assignments and consents, giving the counterparties the opportunity to renegotiate terms with the buyer.[16]

☑ If you can **tax consolidate** the entity into your broader corporate group, and thereby limit the period during which the business and its assets remain exposed to the historical entity. If you can tax consolidate, then you can offer the seller the advantage of an Entity Sale, at the same time you as the buyer obtain the benefit of an asset acquisition.

☑ If the individuals behind the seller have the **financial means to 'make good' any issues** associated with an Entity Sale, i.e. a payment under a warranty or tax indemnity.

☑ If you can secure a significantly better 'deal' from an entity (versus an asset) purchase. For example, if the seller is prepared to pass on some of the tax saving they get from an Entity Sale in the form of a lower purchase price.

Case Study

Tom has run his legal practice as a sole proprietor for over 30 years, but he also has a company that owns the business name and is the registrant for the business' website domain name.

Angela offers to buy the business assets from Tom personally, including goodwill, but also agrees to acquire the shares in Tom's company to ensure that she ends up with all the intangible assets and branding associated with Tom's business.

From ABN, ASIC and other business database searches, Angela can get comfortable that the company has not traded for decades and is unlikely to come with any nasty surprises.

Your acquisition vehicle

You need to set yourself up legally to maximise the commercial and tax outcomes from the acquisition. This will require professional advice from your tax lawyer and accountant. You should also involve your financier to ensure you can raise any required funding for the chosen structure.

For small business acquisitions, many people adopt a discretionary trust with a company trustee. For larger acquisitions, it is common to acquire the assets into a new company (a **Bid Co**). A Bid Co is likely to be a wholly owned subsidiary of an existing company group.

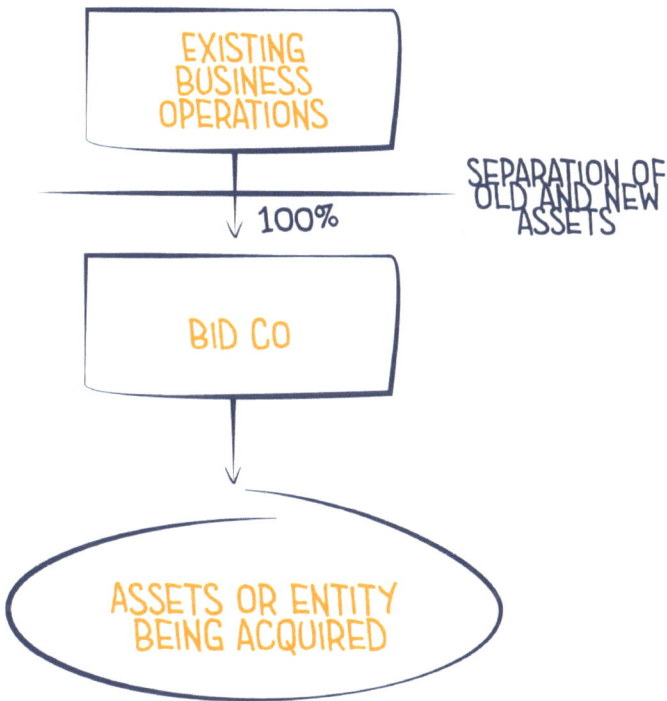

We recommend that all buyers set up a **new entity** specifically to acquire the business or shares (**Bid Co**). This will quarantine any issues you may encounter with the new business from your existing business assets and operations.

You should also consider the nature of the assets you are acquiring and whether this justifies a **multi-entity approach**. For example, if you are acquiring any real estate, it may be preferable to acquire this into a trust structure, separate from the entity in which you will conduct the business.

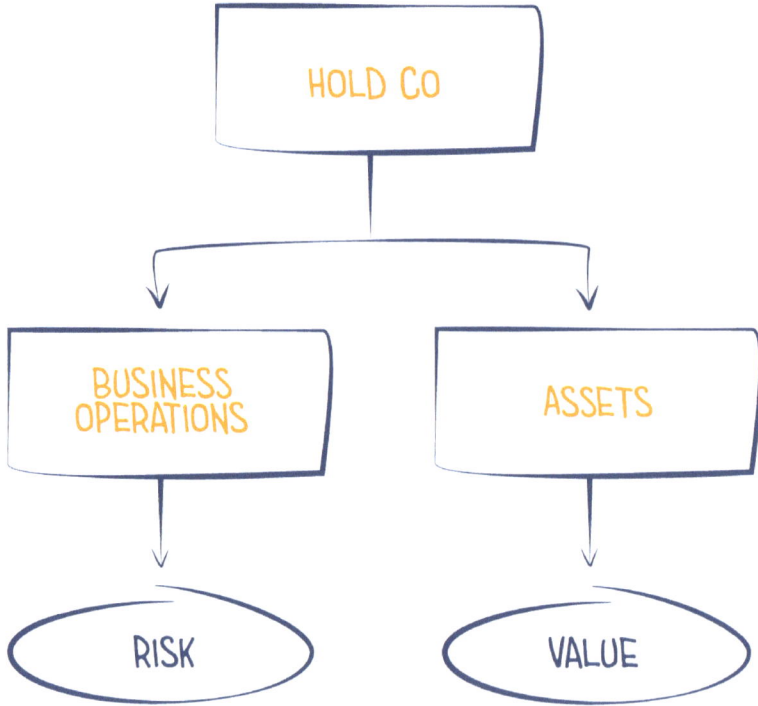

Be aware that for an asset acquisition, the use of multiple entities can complicate the GST treatment of the transaction.

Case Study

Angela had been running both her existing Adelaide and Sydney offices from the one legal entity, being a company trustee for a fixed unit trust.

To quarantine any unforeseen risks associated with Tom's business, she will set up a new entity to carry on the Sydney operations. After settling on the purchase of Tom's practice, Angela intends to then roll over her existing Sydney client base to this new entity.

Tax considerations for buyers

A prospective buyer must seek advice on the tax implications of the proposed transactions as this will have long-lasting implications over the life of the business. This includes a complete understanding of any income tax,[17] capital gains tax, GST, payroll tax and other duty and tax considerations.

We could write an entire book on the tax issues associated with business sales and acquisitions. Set out below is a selection of some of the more common issues.

Apportionment of the sale/purchase price

You need to be aware of the natural tension that typically exists between a buyer and a seller around the tax treatment of the transaction:

- From a buyer's perspective, allocating as much of the purchase price to **revenue assets** (such as plant and inventory) is advantageous because **income tax deductions** will usually be available for the amount paid for these assets; and

- Whereas, from a seller's perspective, allocating as little of the purchase price to revenue assets (e.g. attributing 'written down value' to plant and the lower of cost or market value to inventory) is advantageous. This is because any assessable 'balancing charges' will be minimised, and the balance of the purchase price can be attributed to **capital assets** like goodwill, that may benefit from **CGT concessions**.

The parties can choose to tackle this tension in the Sale Contract, which can **specifically allocate** the purchase price to various assets. Alternatively, the agreement can **remain silent** on the issue, with each party left to find a 'reasonable basis' for the allocation they adopt.

Caution should be taken with the later approach – because if one party relies on an independent third-party valuation of a particular asset, and the other does not get a valuation, the Tax Office can penalise the party who failed to get the independent evidence to support their allocation. So, if you do buy or sell assets without apportioning the purchase price in the Sale Contract, make sure you get a valuation to support the allocation you adopt, no matter what side of the transaction you are on.

Case Study

Given the relatively small amount of tangible assets in Tom's business, Angela is happy to agree in the sale contract that she will acquire any plant and equipment for its written down value.

This meant that most of the sale price will be attributed to 'goodwill'. Tom can then treat this as a capital amount on which he qualifies for various small business CGT concessions. This means that Tom will pay no tax on the sale.

From Angela's perspective, the bulk of the sale price will be 'capital' in nature and therefore not deductible to Angela. However, because Tom will continue as a consultant to the business, Angela can negotiate a more favourable purchase price. Angela will also be able to claim a tax deduction for Tom's future consulting remuneration.

Sale of a GST 'going concern'

The GST treatment of the transaction is largely an issue for the seller. However, it can also have significant impacts for the buyer.

First, **GST is not payable on the purchase of equity** in an entity, (i.e. shares or units). This means the seller of the equity cannot charge GST, and the buyer cannot claim an input tax credit.[18] One flow-on implication of this is that any GST on supplies associated with the transaction, for example, adviser fees, do **not** give rise to GST input tax credits. You may think this is straight forward, but what if you have not settled on the acquisition structure until well into the deal? Can you claim all or part of the input tax credits up to that point? What if the deal does not end up proceeding? Do you then need to go back and make appropriate adjustments?

There can be several potential GST outcomes for an **Asset Purchase**. The default position is that **GST does apply to the supply of the business** from the seller to the buyer. The seller should start from this premise and treat the sale as a **taxable supply**.

This means the buyer will need to initially fund the additional GST paid to the seller, and then recoup this cash back from the Tax Office via its next Business Activity Statement (**BAS**). Practically, this means you must fund an additional 10% on top of the agreed purchase price for a period. Depending on the state in which the business operates, stamp duty may also be payable on the additional GST component, resulting in additional duty.

The seller and buyer may have the option to treat the transaction as a *GST-free* sale and purchase of a **going concern**. Note that the transaction itself must first meet the criteria to **qualify** for this treatment, and then the parties must both **agree** to adopt this treatment. Whether a transaction qualifies is not always obvious,[19] and a seller may simply refuse to adopt this treatment – applying this exemption is still a matter of negotiation and agreement between the parties.

Be aware, if you are buying only **part** of the seller's business, or you are buying **different parts** of the business into **different entities**, then you are unlikely to qualify for going concern treatment.

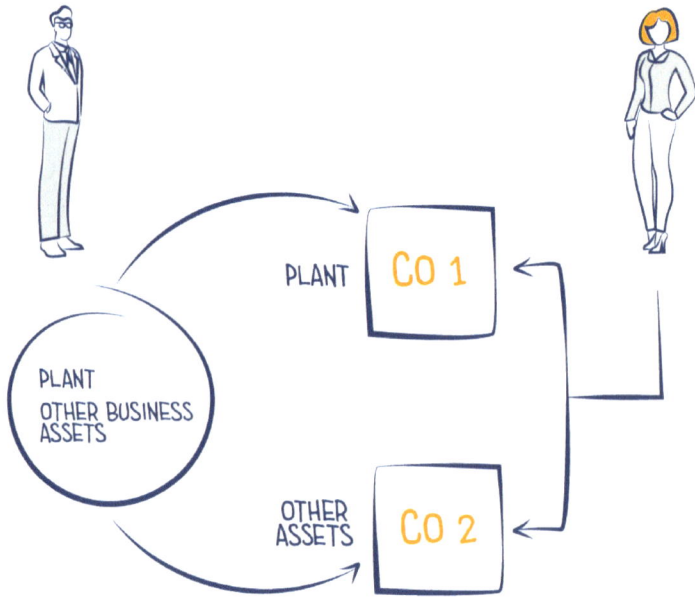

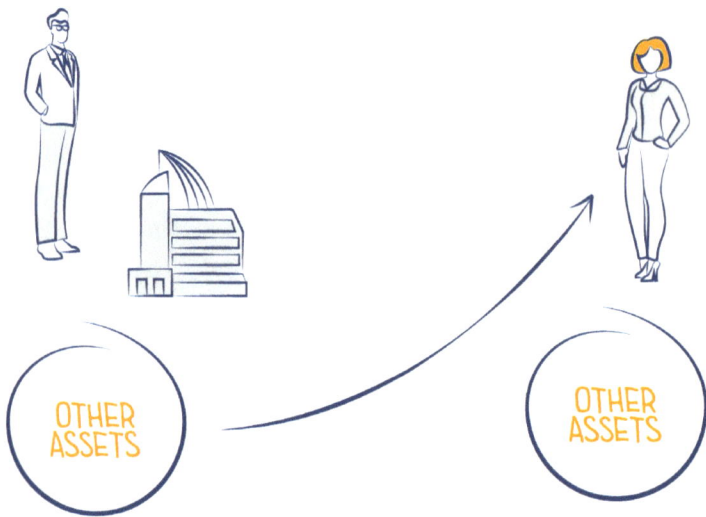

Case Study

As Angela is taking over the whole of Tom's business into a single entity, there is no question about whether the transaction qualifies for the GST going concern exemption.

Tom owns the office from which the business operates, and Angela is not acquiring this real estate. However, the transaction will include Tom granting Angela a lease over the office as from settlement.

A couple of administrative employees will also not join Angela.

Overall, Angela will still acquire a 'complete' operational business from Tom. The parties therefore agree to treat the sale as a GST going concern, and Tom does not need to charge GST on the purchase price.

Stamp and other acquisition duties

Stamp or transaction duties are a state-based tax, and therefore the treatment varies depending on where the business is carried on and where its assets are located.[20]

Currently no state imposes duty on the transfer of **shares** – unless the company holds underlying dutiable property (e.g. real property) over a threshold value. Some states have abolished duty on the transfer of business assets, while others still impose duty on aspects of these transactions.

As buyer, you will need advice on the duty implications of your transaction.

Case Study

Given Tom's business is based solely in Sydney, the transaction falls under the Duties Act 1997 (NSW) and Revenue NSW.

NSW abolished stamp duty on business assets (other than real property business assets) as from 1 July 2016.

However, a nominal duty may still be payable if the business sale includes a transfer of a lease and goods. The nominal duty payable is $10 and is payable on the sale of business agreement and transfer of the lease.

In this case, no duty is payable by Angela on the transaction.

Tax consolidation

Tax consolidation is a complex area, but it can have major implications for the tax-efficiency of an **entity acquisition**.

Put simply, tax consolidation can have the effect of spreading the acquisition cost of the **shares** among the underlying **business assets** of the entity acquired. The outcome is that the buyer effectively gets 'asset acquisition' tax outcomes in the context of a share acquisition. This is best illustrated by example.

Example:

Let's say the seller has a company with two assets, an item of plant with a written-down value of $0 and a market value of $100, and stock with a manufacturing cost of $60 and a wholesale value of $100.

The buyer acquires the company for its market value of $200.

If the buyer was not able to consolidate the new company into their group, then a later sale of the plant for $100 would give rise to a taxable balancing charge of $100 ($100 - $0 = $100).

But if the new company was consolidated, the acquisition value attributed to the plant of $100 would be 'pushed-down' to the plant, increasing its tax value to its market value of $100. A sale of the plant after consolidation would then not give rise to a taxable balancing charge ($100 - $100 = $0).

The same applies to the item of stock. Absent consolidation, the sale of the stock for $100 would give rise to a profit of $40 ($100 - $60 = $40). But after consolidation, the acquisition value of the stock of $100 would be pushed-down to step-up the value of the stock to its market value of $100. A sale of the stock for say $150 would then only give rise to a profit of $50 ($150 - $100 = $50).

In summary, tax consolidation can remove some of the *tax inefficiencies* (i.e. unfairness) of an entity transaction for the buyer. You should consider these issues prior to entering any formal documentation to acquire an **entity**, as it may require some careful pre-planning.

11

Steps in the Acquisition Process

As a prospective buyer, you will generally mirror the transaction steps followed by the seller.

Managers and advisers should be engaged to help address the following threshold questions:

- ☑ Is the business **affordable**?

- ☑ Is the whole or only a part of the business **attractive**?

- ☑ What immediate **concerns** spring to mind?

- ☑ What is the most advantageous way to **structure** the transaction?

You may also want to consider having your own 'pitch document' that sets out what your business does and why the purchase makes sense. Quite often a seller will not just be looking for the best price for their business. They will also be looking to find a **safe set of hands** for their clients and an effective workplace for their employees. All things being equal, the more attractive you are as a buyer, the better deal you will be able to negotiate with the seller.

The EOI and exclusivity

When you respond to an EOI request as a prospective buyer, you should make every effort to keep things flexible and subject to your due diligence findings.

Most people go into a bid process feeling that they are doing the seller a favour by responding, but this is seldom the case. If the business is of **quality**, you will not be the only prospective buyer genuinely interested. If you want to secure the business, and at the right price and terms, then you need to 'sell yourself' to the seller. Many successful entrepreneurs adopt the attitude that 'you can never pay too much for a quality business...'

Once you communicate a baseline price or value for the business (in the non-binding offer or otherwise), again it should demonstrate flexibility and openness to potentially *increasing* your bid price based on your due diligence findings. In this way, if your baseline price is low (from the seller's perspective), you still have a chance to remain engaged in the process, rather than being prematurely disqualified because of a perception of inflexibility or 'bargain hunting'.

As a prospective buyer, you and your advisers should look for innovative ways to **be creative** in the purchase process to **differentiate your bid**. The more options you create for a seller, many of which the seller is unlikely to have considered themselves, the better placed you will be to effectively take over the sale process, relative to other prospective buyers.

Once again, as a prospective buyer you should attempt to secure **exclusivity** with the seller, even for a brief period, to relieve some of the competitive tension that naturally arises from multiple bidders being involved in the process. The best way to secure exclusivity is to **bring something original to the seller** in the form of deal structure. In a competitive bidding situation, simply threatening to pull out unless you get exclusivity will likely see you excluded from the process.

Case Study

As someone experienced in tax law, Angela is able to assist Tom understand the different tax-outcomes that could arise from the sale, and guide Tom towards an Asset Sale with apportionment that will allow Tom to qualify for various CGT concessions – and therefore pay no tax on the deal.

By demonstrating that Tom will pay no tax on the sale, Angela is able to negotiate a lower headline price.

These discussions also allow Angela to develop a rapport with Tom that effectively excluded any other potential buyers entering the race.

Due diligence, checklists, and reports

As a prospective buyer you should take your time, asking all relevant questions to obtain as much information as possible about the business.

You and your advisers should be using every interaction with the seller (and their employees and advisers) to gain information about the business, other potential buyers, and what the seller truly values. This is not always the highest price.

All available **source documents** should be closely reviewed, including invoices and bank statements, because they will prove (or disprove) assertions or views being expressed by the seller. They will also give you a deeper understanding of the true dynamics of the business and its potential value.

There are several tools available to assist you with your due diligence review, including using a comprehensive **Due Diligence Checklist and Questionnaire**, reviewing proposed **warranties** and **indemnities** against due diligence findings, and appointing a co-ordinator or manager of the due diligence process. The manager of this process must then execute the process in a structured, methodical, and organised way, to minimise the risk that critical information is missed.

Case Study

The due diligence process followed by Angela is relatively simple and short. Tom's business is simple from an asset and operations perspective.

The main things Angela is looking to understand included identifying the key clients and the amount of revenue they generate, and the status of the employees.

Angela recognises that there will be less value in Tom's practice if he relies on a few key clients for a large portion of his turnover. Fortunately, Angela' due diligence reveals that most of Tom's work comes through his website from targeted articles addressing current issues. There are a few ongoing clients, but these are larger organisations that are more likely to transition across to a new owner.

Because of the relative importance of Tom's website for generating work, Angela makes further enquiries about ownership of the domain, hosting and backup.

From her enquiries about employees Angela discovers that most have been at the firm for a short period, i.e. there has been consistent and high staff turnover. This indicates to Angela that any client relationship is likely to be dependent on Tom, and that existing staff may not presently have strong reasons to be committed to and stay with the business.

Prepare a Due Diligence Report

We highly recommend preparing a **Due Diligence Report** as a natural and necessary part of every robust due diligence exercise. This report typically:

- ☑ Identifies the **nature and scope** of the due diligence performed, and the universe of information reviewed;

- ☑ Clearly sets out all the **material findings**, including price-sensitive discoveries;

- ☑ Identifies **areas of risk** or exposure to potential liability, along with recommendations on how such risks or exposures can be managed or mitigated, including through proposed warranties and indemnities;

- ☑ Articulates the **business' strengths** (including what makes it unique or different), and areas for improvement; and

- ☑ Contains an overall **'go' or 'no go' recommendation**, along with reasons for that recommendation.

Case Study

Prior to proceeding with the acquisition, Angela prepares a summary of her findings from her due diligence investigations into Tom's practice. Angela then meets with Tim to discuss her findings and to reach a 'go' or 'no go' decision.

Tim agrees with Angela that the business represents a good opportunity to increase revenue and profits in Sydney. However, Tim also forces Angela to focus on some of the obvious risks that Angela was glossing over, including the potential loss of staff soon after the acquisition, and the fact that several of the larger clients are likely to be attached personally to Tom.

At the price Angela has been able to negotiate, together with the high level of vendor finance, Tim agrees with Angela that on balance the deal is a good one, and Angela should proceed.

Keep a lid on your advisers

Your external advisers should be closely monitored and managed, so they only invest as much time and energy in the process as is reasonably necessary or appropriate.

Over-investment of your advisers' time means you are spending more than you should, while an under-investment of advisers' time could mean that not enough guidance and assistance is being provided. This can be a difficult balance to manage, especially if this is your first transaction.

A lot of advisers attempt to 'take over' the acquisition process. You should not allow this to happen. You must remain in overall control, and retain responsibility from beginning to end. If you are not comfortable doing this, then you are probably not ready to take on an acquisition. This applies to SME acquisitions, as well as those by much larger enterprises. In fact, larger enterprises are more prone to abdicating responsibility to external advisers, rather than internal executives taking a lead role.

Look for indications of true value

As a prospective buyer you should use the due diligence process to discover a business' **true value**. It is important that you remain disciplined and unemotional – being prepared to walk away if true value falls short of what you are willing and able to pay. On the other hand, if you discover more value than you anticipated, you should be willing to increase your bid price to reflect this.

Case Study

During Angela's due diligence of Tom's practice, Angela discovers that a large portion (over 60%) of the work coming to the practice originates from website enquires. These enquiries are driven by blog content that has been published over many years (i.e. 'evergreen' content).

Angela also discovers that the practice is well known among the local community of Potts Point, and benefits from a steady-stream of property law enquires to the main telephone line that could be handled by a junior associate.

This was value that Angela did not expect to find. She now knows to take particular care to ensure the assignment of the website domains, the main telephone number, and the 'brand' known in the local community.

Negotiating the Sale Contract

Regardless of whether a **share** purchase agreement or **Asset Purchase** agreement is being used, as a prospective buyer you must negotiate an appropriate set of **warranties** and **indemnities** into the transaction agreement, to manage and/or mitigate any potential risks or liabilities of the acquisition.

Other means of contractually managing risk and potential exposure include **post-completion adjustments**, **restraints of trade** and potential **clawbacks**.

Warranties and indemnities

We have already discussed the importance of negotiating satisfactory warranties and indemnities. As noted, the issue of warranties and indemnities is going to be a much bigger issue in the context of an Entity Purchase. This is because you are not just buying the business as it exists at settlement, but you are also buying the seller's '**history of operations**' that will come with the legal entity. You are buying the seller's 'cupboard' that may come with hidden skeletons.

The purpose of warranties and indemnities is to give you the ability to go back to the seller and ask for an adjustment to what you have paid to reflect the cost of any skeletons you discover down the track.

What is a tax indemnity?

The liability for tax falls on the **entity** operating the business. Our laws give the Australian Tax Office (and various state revenue offices) the right to review what tax was paid in previous years, and demand that any underpayment of tax in a prior year be paid now.[21]

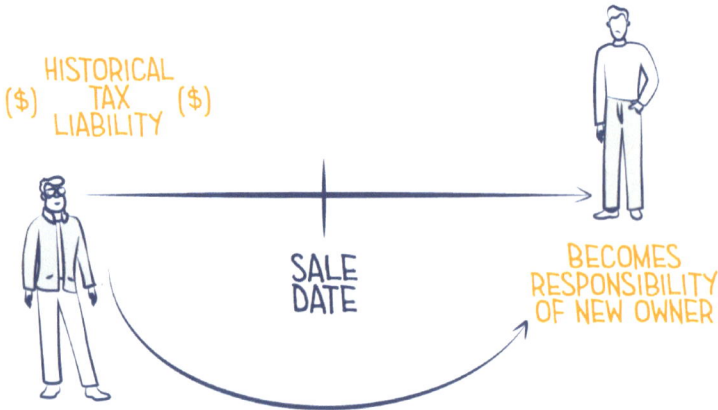

So, a buyer taking over an entity (i.e. in an **Entity Sale**) is taking over responsibility for any tax that may have been underpaid in a previous year. This **contingent tax liability** could be very large. In fact, it could be significantly more than the 'net assets' purchased.

To protect against this risk, a buyer should require the seller to provide a **comprehensive indemnity for any tax liabilities** that are imposed on the entity *and that relate to the period prior to the takeover.*

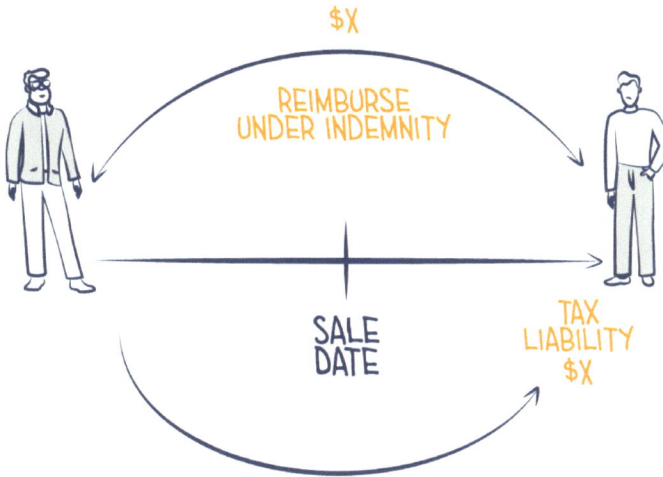

On the other hand, the seller will not want to write a blank cheque for the buyer to simply pay whatever tax is threatened against the entity post-sale. They will want to ensure that the buyer properly objects to any disputed tax liability.

The terms on which the seller provides the tax indemnity, and the buyer undertakes to property manage these historical liabilities, can be included in an appropriately worded '**tax indemnity**'. The tax indemnity may be included in the main body of the Share Purchase Agreement or can be documented in a separate Tax Indemnity Deed.

A comprehensive tax indemnity is not necessary for an Asset Sale, because the historical tax liabilities largely remain with the selling entity. The assets and liabilities acquired by the buyer should not be encumbered by these contingencies.

Securing a reasonable restraint of trade

If you are paying an amount for 'goodwill' (i.e. paying more than the value of the net tangible assets), you must secure a **reasonable commercial restraint of trade** to protect that value.

A well drafted restraint of trade will prevent the seller (and their associates) from **competing** with you after the sale, and thereby stop them 'taking back' the goodwill you have paid for.

As a rule, the law does not like to restrain people from being able to make a living, so the restraint needs to be '**reasonable**'. It will be considered reasonable when it goes only so far as is necessary to protect the **legitimate commercial interests** of the buyer, i.e. to protect what you have paid for.

Obviously, whether a restraint is 'reasonable'[22] depends on the particular facts and circumstances, but there are typically three relevant factors:

- The breadth of the **activities** that are restrained;

- The **period** over which the restraint applies; and

- The **geographical area** where the restraint applies.

The restrained activities

There are many things a seller could do post-sale that would negatively impact the value of what you have bought.

Non-solicitation

A common restraint prohibits the seller from **approaching** or **soliciting** business from existing customers or clients of the business, i.e. the customers you 'bought' from the seller. The concept of 'soliciting' is limited. It relates to the positive acts of the seller in approaching the clients with a view to providing them with goods or services.

A common defence to an accusation of the seller soliciting former clients is that 'the clients approached me'. The onus of proof is on you (the buyer) to prove that the seller did something that amounts to 'solicitation'. Is simply updating their LinkedIn profile, or putting an ad in an industry publication, sufficient to amount to solicitation? Probably not.

Non-dealing

One solution to the difficulty of proving the positive act of solicitation is to specifically **prohibit** the seller from dealing with former clients, i.e. providing goods or services to a specific list of clients.

This is a very effective form of restraint because it is usually quite clear if a seller has breached the prohibition and there will be objective evidence in the business records of the seller that they have dealt with a former client.

However, this prohibition will only be effective for a business that has a **stable list of clients**, for example, a professional services business. It will be much less effective for a business that serves a very large number of clients, has anonymous clients, or has a clients base that turns over on a consistent basis, for example, a retail business.

Non-competition

A more comprehensive restraint would prohibit the seller from **competing** with your business. This not only stops them from soliciting or providing goods or services to your existing clients, but also from **running a business** that competed with you for *new* clients.

To be effective, a non-competition restraint requires a clear **definition of the 'business'** the seller is prohibited from carrying on. This is usually defined with reference to the nature and extent of the business carried on by the seller for a period prior to settlement (usually 2 years). If you significantly change the nature of the business after settlement, then the additional activities may not fall within the restraint.

A non-competition restraint usually requires some **geographical** or **market limit** to be considered commercially reasonable, as discussed below.

Other restrained activities

Because the seller knows so much about the business, there are other things they could do that would cause serious damage to the assets you have purchased. For this reason, other restrained activities should include:

- ☑ Approaching those persons who have historically **referred** work to the business. This is a different group to clients, in that the referrers may not be clients themselves, but a large portion of the value of the business may be reliant on regular referrals from these people.

- ☑ Approaching or engaging your **employees**. The employees are talent you have 'paid for' as part of the purchase. Finding well trained and quality employees is costly. Losing key employees (or several employees) could seriously impact the viability of the business.

- ☑ Interfering with the terms of supply to your business. The **supplier** relationships are also valuable, with potentially unique and confidential aspects.

The more broadly the restrained activities are defined, the more likely a court will find that the restraint is unenforceable. However, in the context of a business sale (as opposed to an employment context), courts are more willing to uphold even a very broad array of restrained activities.

The duration of the restraint

A restraint cannot last forever. It can only last so long as is **commercially reasonable and necessary** to secure the value the buyer has paid for.

It is common practice for restraints to be somewhere between 3 to 5 years in duration. This appears arbitrary, but it is not. This timeframe usually aligns closely with the 'profit multiples' adopted in calculating the purchase price of private enterprises.

For example, if the price was based on a '4-times' multiple of adjusted earnings, then a restraint of 4 years post acquisition would reflect the period over which the buyer could be expected to earn profits approximating what they paid. This seems proportionate and therefore 'reasonable'.

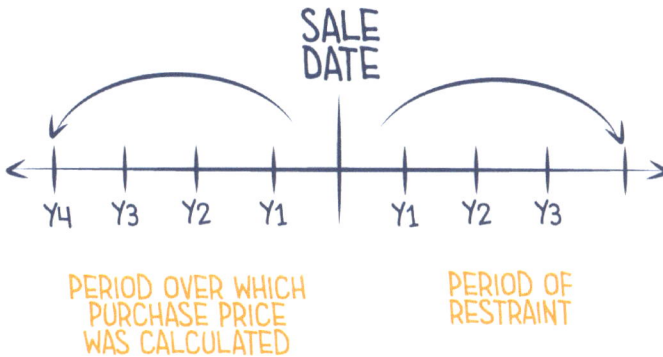

The longer the duration of the restraint, the more likely it is to be declared void by a court as unreasonable, e.g. 6 years is more likely to be held 'unreasonable' than 3 years.

Another factor that will be considered when assessing the reasonableness of the restraint is the timeframe it would reasonably take for the buyer to **establish a relationship** with the clients. For a business that sees clients very often, the restraint is likely to be shorter than a business that only sees clients every few years.

The 'area' over which the restraint applies

You buy a business with a particular 'market footprint'. This is the **geographic** or **demographic area** over which the business earns its profits. A reasonable **non-competition restraint** is one that aligns with this geographic or demographic footprint of the business that you have purchased.

Traditionally, buyers have set the **restrained area** for a non-competition restraint as a **radial geographic distance** from the business premises. While this works for a local business serving a local market, many businesses no longer operate in this way.

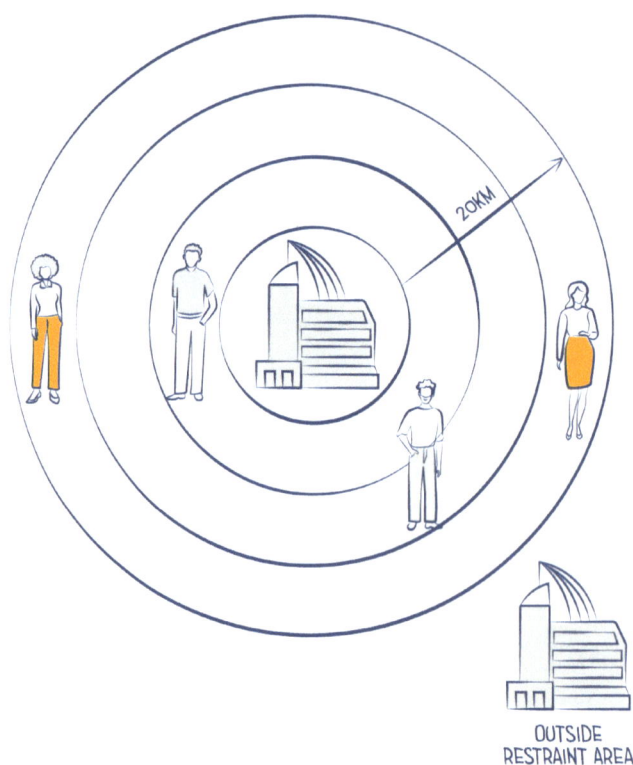

OUTSIDE
RESTRAINT AREA

As a buyer you should define the restrained area as any '**market**' in which the business operated during the period prior to the purchase. This will capture the immediate geographic area around the business' location(s), and any areas or demographic markets in which the business has earned its revenue.

As more businesses operate on a 'virtual' basis and service markets globally, adopting a definition of this nature is more important.

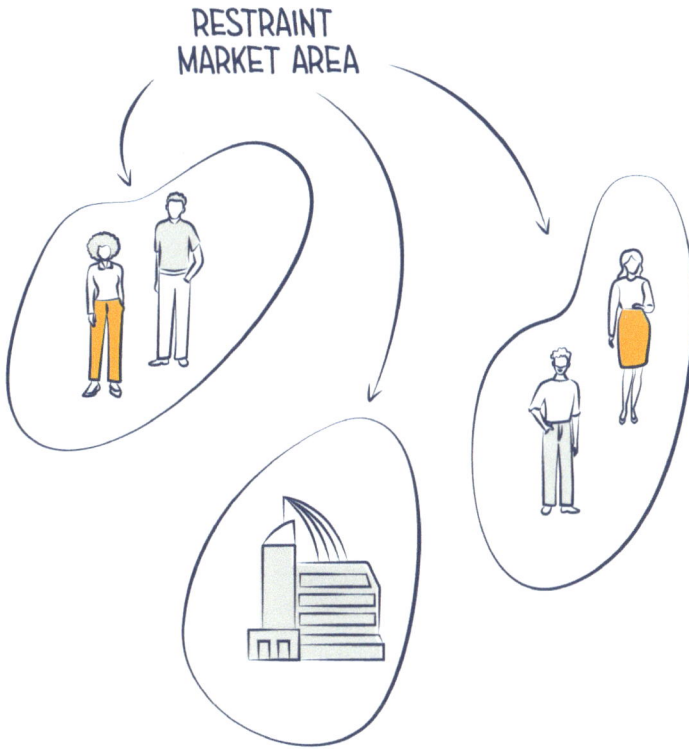

RESTRAINT
MARKET AREA

Note: In the case of a **non-dealing restraint** that relates to a list of clients, it is not necessary (or appropriate) to also impose a geographic limitation on the restraint. These clients should be off-limits irrespective of where they are located.

Case Study

Tom is the only proprietor of the practice, and the practice is closely associated with Tom and his personal brand, so it is critical for Angela to secure a strong and broad restraint.

As a large portion of the practice's income comes from website enquires from all over Sydney, Angela needs to secure a broad **non-competition restraint** that prevents Tom from re-establishing a Sydney-wide web-presence.

Angela also needs to secure an explicit **non-dealing restraint** for the key clients and referrers that send regular business to the practice.

In addition to the restraints, Angela also includes a **positive obligation** on Tom to introduce Angela to the key clients and referrers, and assist Angela establish a positive and enduring relationship with them.

Drafting tips and techniques

While restraints are always open to challenge (on the ground that they are unreasonable), as a prospective buyer you can use certain **drafting techniques** to strengthen your restraint and mitigate the risks of it being successfully challenged.

Restraining the right parties

Too often restraints that have been drafted well from a technical perspective simply **fail to restrain the right people**. For example, if you are buying a business from a company, and the restraint applies to the 'vendor', it is the company that will be restrained. The company may be wound up shortly after the sale, and your restraint is worthless. In this context, the people you will be concerned about are the directors and owners of the vendor.

The next mistake people make is extending the restraint to cover the directors and owners of the vendor – but then failing to make those persons a **legal party** to the sale contract. The parties you wish to bind legally need to sign the document!

Direct and indirect activities

Even if you properly identify the relevant individuals who need to be restrained and make them a legal party to the sale contract, this may still not be enough to protect your goodwill.

It doesn't take too much imagination to get around a direct restraint on an individual. For example, they could 'assist' a family member start or expand a business that would otherwise breach the restraint.

For this reason, your restraint must not only prohibit them directly doing the prohibited activities, but also *indirectly* doing them through or on behalf of someone else. This wording needs to be carefully drafted to be effective, but it is very necessary to craft an effective restraint.

Ladder clauses

A restraint will only be effective if it is 'reasonable'. There is another legal principle that works in tandem with this, namely that the unreasonable element will be 'struck out' by the court. If, when the unreasonable part is struck-out, the restraint makes no sense, then the whole restraint can be void.

To deal with these principles, lawyers have invented several drafting techniques. The main idea is to construct the restraint in several discrete and self-contained 'blocks' so that if a block is struck-out by the court, the rest of the restraint remains effective.

One such technique that often causes confusion is the **'ladder' clause**. A ladder clause looks like this:

The seller must not, for the longer of the following periods, do any of the restrained activities:

36 months from settlement;

24 months from settlement; and

12 months from settlement.

The idea here is that the court can 'strike-out' say *'36 months from settlement'* if it thinks that is too long for a reasonable restraint. Because of how the clause is drafted, the remaining restraint periods still apply. In this case, the 'longest' period would then be 24 months, and this would remain enforceable.

The key to such clauses is that they should not be uncertain (in the normal contractual principles sense) and should reflect a genuine attempt by the parties to establish a reasonable and clearly defined restraint, rather than leaving it up to the court to define it.

In some states and in some contexts, this technique is no longer necessary. But it remains a good idea to ensure the restraint has the best chance of being upheld.

Clawbacks and liquidated damages

Another drafting technique you should use as a buyer is linking a particular restrained activity (such as the seller breaching a non-dealing restraint) with a **clawback** of a portion of the purchase price you have paid.

This technique avoids the need for you to prove you have suffered damage or loss, because you have agreed with the seller that if the seller does something (e.g. deals with a client after settlement) they will be contractually obliged to pay you an agreed amount. If you calculated the purchase price on a multiple of, say, 2 times revenue, and the seller took back a client who had spent $15,000 with the business in a previous year, then the amount to be paid back by the seller would be say $30,000.

Signing and Settlement

Business as usual

There is often a time gap between executing the purchase contract and settling the acquisition. As the buyer, you should try and keep this gap to a minimum, as the seller is likely to 'switch-off' to some degree after securing the sale.

You should also monitor the actions of the seller and business to ensure they are adhering to the '**business as usual**' undertaking in the contract. It may be that the seller needs to obtain your prior written consent to take certain actions outside the usual course of business during this period. If approached for consent, you should ensure you understand the full consequences of what the seller is contemplating, and not be shy to ask for additional information before making your decision.

You should also use this time to **plan for a smooth transition**. Ideally you will have included provisions in the contract that enable you to have access to financial and operational information for the business. You can use this to prepare a plan for the day you take over.

Conditions precedent

As noted in an earlier chapter, it is common in both Asset Sales and Entity Sales for the transaction to be conditional on certain things being procured or done prior to settlement.

Usually, these conditions are for the benefit of the buyer, and it will be up to you to ensure that they are satisfied, or voluntarily waived.

Depending on how the deal has been structured, you may have agreed to enter a conditional binding contract to purchase the business – subject to undertaking '**satisfactory due diligence**'. A well-advised vendor will place a tight timeframe on this process, and you will need to be ready with your team to quickly and thoroughly undertake enquires and reach a go/no-go decision on the acquisition.

If a condition precedent is for your benefit as buyer, and the vendor has not been able to satisfy the condition prior to the agreed settlement date, think carefully before agreeing to waive the condition. In most cases it will be better to agree with the vendor to defer settlement until the condition has been satisfied. If you waive the condition, or enter an informal arrangement to deal with the issue after settlement, you may find it very difficult (if not impossible) to actually get the condition satisfied following settlement after the vendor has their cash.

You also need to be careful that your acquisition team and advisers do not go to sleep following the signing of the purchase contract and before settlement. There are often a lot of formalities to be taken care of during this interim phase to prepare for a successful and timely settlement, followed by a smooth transition. You should prepare and maintain a **Settlement Checklist**, and ensure there is clear accountability for getting things done.

Post settlement matters

While many of the following points are obvious, it is surprisingly common to see buyers fail to take some basic steps after settling on the business to facilitate a smooth transition. You need to start the new journey 'on the right foot' by being organised and prepared. Ironically, many buyers fail to take even the most basic post-acquisition steps to ensure they have secured proper ownership of the assets they have just purchased.

Organisation is a key element to continued success, and the following steps will help you remain organised as the new owner of your business.

Insurance

It is essential that you confirm all necessary **insurance** coverage is in place for the assets and activities of the business.

Your insurance should be put in place well before completion of the purchase. You must understand when 'risk' in the assets and operations passes to you under the sale contract. This point in time is often from when you **sign the contract** rather than settle. You need to have insurance in place from this point in time.

We strongly suggest you engage an **experienced insurance broker** to provide you with written advice on what insurances you will need, given the nature of what you are acquiring, as well as the limits that you should adopt. Insurance is something you should not try to do yourself. Just following what the seller had in place prior to the sale is no guarantee you will have all the insurance you need moving forward.

Banking

Confirm all necessary **banking** arrangements and authorities are in place as soon as possible following a change in ownership. This includes credit card merchant accounts so you can continue to process payments from the date of settlement.

If you are acquiring the seller's **entity**, then you must ensure you are given control over all the entity's bank accounts from completion. You should also ensure that all pre-existing operating authorities are reviewed and cancelled if necessary. The last thing you want is the vendor dipping into your account following completion.

If you are buying **assets** into an entity you already control (or that you have set up for the acquisition), the banking arrangements for your entity need to be in place well prior to completion, so the business can continue operating.

Some customers will continue to remit payments to the seller's old bank account for work done after you have taken over. You must ensure you can track these payments, and that the seller is obliged to pass the cash on to you in a short timeframe. Otherwise, you will quickly run out of cash.

Take control of the physical assets

Immediately take 'ownership', **control**, and **responsibility** for all aspects of the business.

Don't assume that certain parts of the business will 'take care of themselves' – they may not. You need to know the location, condition and purpose of all the assets you have purchased, and that they are being properly looked after from the date of settlement.

Ensure the permits and licences are in place

Ensure all permits, licenses, notices, transfers, consents, and approvals have been obtained, made or registered.

From the date of settlement, it is your responsibility to ensure the business remains in compliance with all applicable laws, regulations and contractual and other obligations.

If the business is highly regulated, then you should make obtaining and/ or compliance with any necessary regulatory matters a pre-condition to settlement.

You should maintain a **register** of permits and licences, including key people, expiry dates and any conditions you need to satisfy to continue to qualify to maintain the permit or licence.

Take control of the intangible assets

The physical assets of the business are obvious and often take care of themselves. However, it is very common for the effective ownership and control of intangible assets to be overlooked following settlement.

Have you obtained landlord consent and registered the assignment of leases with the land titles office? Have you updated the ownership of trademarks, patents and registered designs? Have you updated the registrant details for all relevant domain names? Social media accounts can be complex to transfer, as they are often associated with a particular individual. What about telephone and mobile numbers?

Stamping and duties

All states in Australia currently impose duty on the transfer of various categories of assets. Depending on where the business is located, this may have implications for your business purchase. If you do not pay the appropriate duty, then this will compromise your 'title' over those assets.

Some states impose duty on the transfer of 'businesses', while most have abolished this duty. However, even states that have abolished duty on business transfers still maintain duty on the on the transfer of certain 'parts' of a business, such as motor vehicles or commercial property.

You will need to get advice on the duty implications in each state in which the business is carried on, or where it maintains assets.

Getting value for money

Once you own a new business, the hard work is not over; it is just beginning.

One of the most important pieces of 'insurance' you can have in place is maintaining the **value proposition** of what was acquired. As a buyer you can do this by:

- Spending quality time getting to **know new clients or customers**. There is no substitute for genuine, lasting relationships, and it's never too early to start forging them.

- Spending quality time motivating, supporting, integrating, and **retaining key staff**. All staff should be afforded the respect and responsibility that they deserve and expect. All roles should be clearly defined and delineated, so there is no confusion as to roles and responsibilities.

- **Addressing any issues of conflict**, whether at the policy, process or employee level, early, fairly and transparently.

- Eliminating those aspects of the business that are not working and **focusing your energy and resources** on the aspects of the business that are working.

- **Honouring** and **respecting** the **culture** and **heritage** of the acquired business as much as possible, while integrating it into your existing business (in the case of a merger), or while introducing new ownership and/or management.

Regrettably, all too often we see wonderful businesses with great histories stripped of identity and purpose overnight by over-zealous new owners or managers, influenced more by unchecked ego and pride than by good, objective judgment.

Start with a simple 'Transition Plan'

There are many books and complex theories about how to run a business well. Many of these new theories say that having a good business plan and marketing plan are a waste of time. While it is true that a static business plan is unlikely to be enough for longer term success, in the context of an acquisition, a simple business or 'transition' plan is a good place to start.

Starting with the (existing) IM provided by the seller during the acquisition process, develop a simple **Business Plan** to take the business forward in the period immediately post takeover. Marketing plans, budgets and forecasts are also very important parts of ensuring sufficient management, control and oversight of the business are in place during the period of transition.

The main point here is that starting the planning process after the acquisition is complete is probably starting too late. You need to have a plan in place as to what you are going to do with the business well before you take over. This can be a good reason to have a period between when you sign the sale contract and when you settle on the business, so you have time to get your head in the right place and hit the ground running.

12

Funding an Acquisition

There are different potential sources of funding for a business acquisition. As a buyer, you should consider all of them.

Equity

The simplest form of funding is straight '**equity**'. For a small business acquisition, this may be your savings. For acquisitions by larger groups, equity may come in the form of retained earnings or additional equity raised from investors.

As a rule, equity is the **most expensive form of funding**. This is because the providers of equity take the highest risk. If things go wrong, equity holders are the last to get paid any income or a return of their capital, i.e. they take the 'first loss'. To compensate for this higher risk, equity providers expect commensurate higher returns – they want a piece of the action.[23]

Long-term average returns on equity in Australian public markets are around 8% p.a.[24] Data for returns on equity invested in private companies is harder to find. Target returns on equity for professional private equity investors is said to be around 20% to 30% p.a., which represents a significant premium to public market returns. This is a more realistic indication of the 'cost of equity' for private and corporate acquirers.

In summary, all things being equal, you should minimise the extent of equity that you use to fund your acquisitions.

Case Study

Like most small business owners, Angela has no choice but to invest her own equity in buying Tom's legal practice.

Given Angela operates her existing business through a unit trust, this equity represents Angela's after-tax savings.

Most small businesses are funded by the savings of the proprietors.

Debt

Another source of funding is debt. Debt takes priority over equity with respect to the payment of a periodic return (i.e. interest) and the repayment of the original capital (i.e. the principal). Debt is therefore seen as a lower risk investment, with commensurate lower expected returns when compared with equity, (at least this is the theory!).

The problem with debt for most small to medium sized buyers is getting access to it.

Trading banks are the traditional providers of debt to Australian enterprises. It is well documented that these banks are reluctant to provide debt to SMEs without **security over real property**.[25] This is particularly the case when the debt it to be used to acquire a new business. For those SMEs able to access debt, the interest rate spread above the risk-free rate is around twice that paid by larger companies.[26]

Graph 2

Interest Rate Spreads on Business Debt

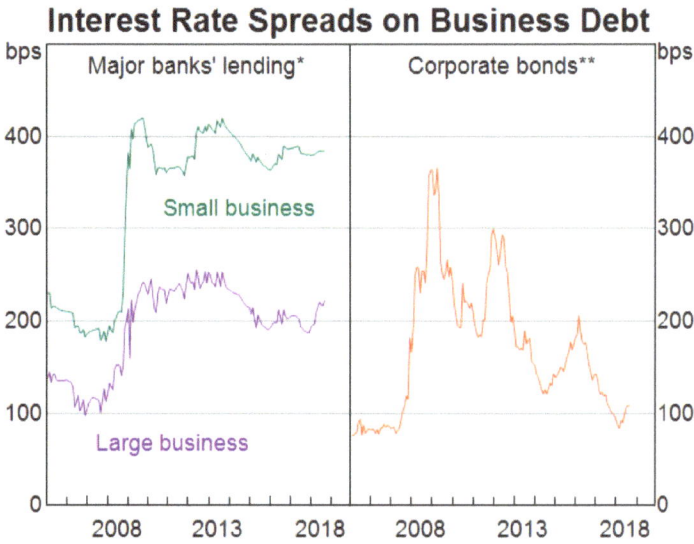

* Rates on outstanding lending; spread to cash rate; small business loans are defined as those below $2 million
** Five-year secondary market non-resource corporate bond spreads over AGS
Sources: APRA; Bloomberg; Financial Reports; RBA; UBS AG, Australian Branch

Larger businesses have more options when it comes to raising debt for acquisitions. This includes traditional debt from trading banks, as well as raising debt directly from investors by issuing **corporate bonds** into the public debt markets. The premium over the risk-free rate for corporate bonds has been falling in line with returns more generally, making this an attractive funding source for large corporates.

Equipment finance

One area where SME buyers may have more luck obtaining traditional finance is for equipment. Traditional trading banks and other financial institutions are more likely to provide some level of funding for **tangible items** that have an **identifiable resale market**, such as vehicles and equipment used in mature industries such as professional services, hospitality and transport.

The more unique or bespoke the equipment, the harder it will be to find debt or lease finance.

Case Study

Tom has existing equipment finance for his photocopier and phone system. These finance facilities only have a small number of payments left, so Angela agrees to assume responsibility for the remaining payments on this finance.

In return, Tom agrees to assign the residual right to this equipment to Angela on the final payment being made.

It would not be practical to formally assign these facilities to Angela, and Tom is happy with Angela's contractual indemnity for these obligations in the Sale Contract.

Vendor finance

Perhaps the largest source of funding available to the SME sector is '**vendor finance**'. This is finance provided by the seller of the business to the buyer. No cash changes hands, the seller agrees to acknowledge a debt due from the buyer in part satisfaction of the purchase price.

In many cases this funding is provided at a low rate of interest when compared to other sources or comparable debt, or even interest-free for a period post-acquisition.

Furthermore, many vendors will agree to a **second-ranking security** for this funding behind any funding provided by a traditional trading bank. For this reason, vendor finance often acts as a 'bridge' between traditional debt funding and the equity available to the buyer.

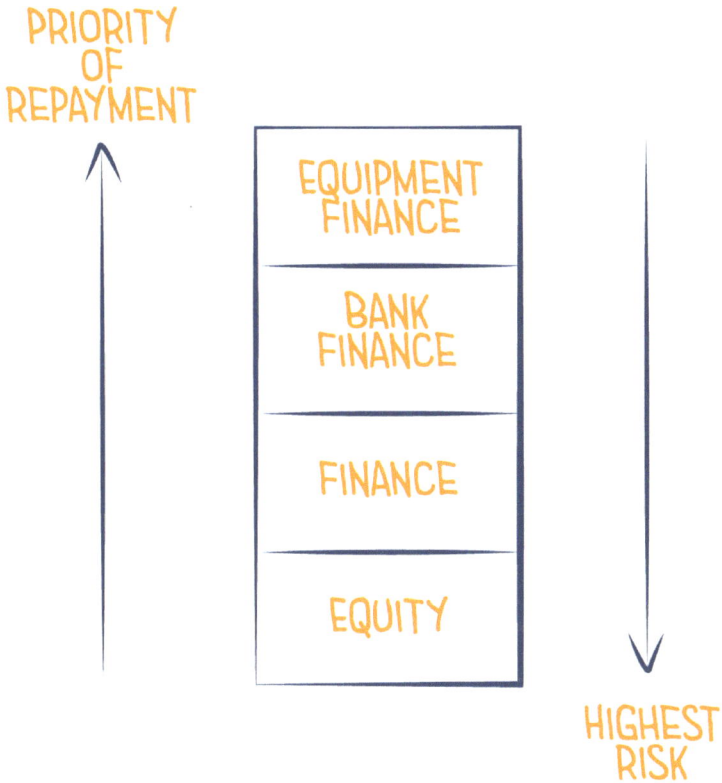

PRIORITY OF REPAYMENT

EQUIPMENT FINANCE

BANK FINANCE

FINANCE

EQUITY

HIGHEST RISK

The reason a vendor is likely to be a competitive source of funding is that they know the risks and benefits of what they are selling. They are also best placed to step back in and protect their debt position should the buyer fail.

When negotiating this funding you should take into consideration the following:

Recognise the *de facto* retention amount

A level of vendor funding can act like a 'retention amount' to cover potential warranty claims and other clawbacks that a buyer makes after settlement. If you have a legitimate claim against the seller during the funding period, the amount can offset and reduce the balance of vendor funding to be repaid.

Set a realistic repayment term

The repayment term for the vendor finance should be set at a level that the business is likely to be able to afford. Remember that any principal repayments will need to be funded 'after-tax', so tax needs to be factored into how much cash you will have available for the principal repayments.

Create an incentive to refinance

If you are the seller providing the vendor finance, you should set the effective interest rate on the funding above what the buyer is paying for their traditional debt, so the buyer has a commercial incentive to swap-out your vendor finance for third party debt as soon as is possible.

If you are the seller, you should limit the length of any interest-free period, and if the buyer falls behind in any repayments, a higher rate of interest should apply to compensate for this.

Ensure the buyer has some 'skin in the game'

If you are the seller, you should seek security over both the buyer's business assets, as well as their personal assets, via a 'director guarantee'. Obviously, if you are the buyer, you should resist this!

From a seller's perspective, the important thing is that the buyer has some **capital at risk** to ensure they remain focused on making the business a success and repaying the vendor finance within the agreed term.

Case Study

A key term for Angela' acquisition of Tom's practice is Tom providing vendor finance for 50% of the purchase price over a 2 year period.

Angela is concerned that Tom will retire prior to transitioning the 'goodwill' in the client base. Therefore, they agree that if Tom ceases working in the business during the 2-year period, then any balance of the unpaid purchase price will be waived. The vendor finance therefore also acted as a 'retention amount' against this possibility.

The funding advantage of larger enterprises

Overall, when it comes to funding acquisitions, larger enterprises have considerably more firepower than SMEs, both from an equity and debt perspective. They have greater access to funding and pay a lower price for it.

Larger enterprises are therefore more able to make strategic acquisitions of quality businesses. If you are building a business to sell, then structuring it to be **attractive to larger businesses** is a sound strategy. You should not overlook the potential for a larger business to see strategic value in what you are selling and be prepared to pay a meaningful premium.

If you are a larger enterprise with access to funding at competitive rates, your growth strategy must include the acquisition of businesses at multiples that are value-accretive from the outset. You should be looking to buy businesses returning 20-30% p.a. ROE at a funding cost sub 8% p.a.

Financial assistance

The *Corporations Act 2001* (Cth) places limits on the ability for a buyer to use the assets of a target company to fund the acquisition of the shares in the target.[27] This is known as '**financial assistance**', because the target company is *assisting the buyer* to buy the target.

Financial assistance is quite common. It is not limited to when the target provides debt to the buyer. It more commonly arises when the buyer is going to provide security over the assets of the target to the financier providing the funding to acquire the shares.

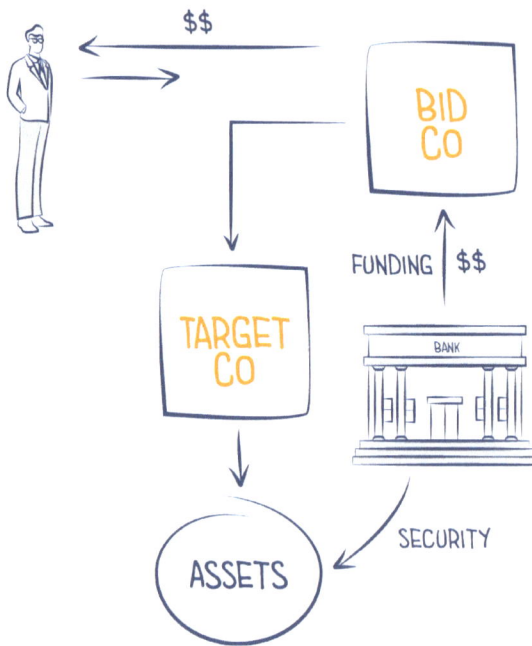

If the financial assistance is not exempt from the prohibition, or it is not approved in the appropriate manner, any person involved in the financial assistance may commit an offence under the *Corporations Act 2001* (Cth). This can include the directors as well as the advisers to the company.[28]

Financial assistance can be quite simply approved by the **shareholders** of the target company passing a **special resolution** in a general meeting.[29]

If any aspect of the funding for an entity acquisition relies on something to be done by the target entity, then you need to obtain specific advice on the potential application of these rules.

13

Selecting the 'Right' Advisers

Whether you are a seller or buyer, selecting the right advisers goes a long way to achieving your desired outcome in the most efficient, practical and painless way. It's worth spending the time upfront to find yourself a proactive and deal-ready team.

Advisers who clearly demonstrate, through actions more than words, that they have an **awareness** of, and a genuine **desire to,** assist you **grow your businesses** are those that add the most value. How do they do this? By proactively introducing you to potential clients, customers and other useful third parties.

Great advisers take a holistic approach. They invest time and energy getting to know your needs and the broader markets in which you conduct your business, (including the competitive landscape). They are open to facilitating your business development activities, through everyday introductions as well as identifying strategic acquisition opportunities.

Engaging a business broker or corporate adviser

Someone needs to take responsibility for and run your sale process. In reality, you are not that person. Do you have the experience and day-to-day capacity to both run your business and a complex sale process? An obvious place to turn is to a business broker, or in the case of larger enterprises, a financial or corporate adviser.

Engaging a broker is not a bad idea, but like all advisers, business brokers come in many different varieties. You need to do your due diligence, and not just focus on 'cost'. A cheap broker may save you a few thousand dollars in commission, but you may end up missing out on hundreds of thousands, or even millions, in a lower sale price. For example, a business broker who does not understand competitive tension, or is too lazy to try to generate and maintain it, will cost you a significant percentage of your business' value.

The 'beauty parade'

The way experienced entrepreneurs choose an adviser is through what is known as a '**beauty parade**'. First, you start with a short list of potential brokers. You can build this short list by talking with your existing advisers, (e.g. your accountant and lawyer), as well as business associates and trade organisations.

You then interview each potential broker and run through a common list of questions:

- First, you want to find out how well they have **prepared for your meeting**. What do they know about your business and the industry you operate in? If they have not prepared for your meeting, chances are they will not be prepared for other aspects of the sale process. Don't let them waste your time.

- Have they **recently sold** any businesses in your industry?

- Have they sold any businesses in any complimentary industries? For example, the industries of your suppliers or customers?

- Out of all the transactions they were entrusted with, what actual transactions have they **concluded**? How many did <u>not</u> conclude, and why not? If they say they have a 100% success rate, they are lying. You want an honest broker, and one that can learn from their prior mistakes.

- What **value did they achieve**, and on what metrics, (i.e. multiples of profits, revenue, etc.)? They will struggle with this question if they have not actually sold anything recently, or in your industry. Don't take 'confidentiality' as an excuse. You are not looking for names, merely some numbers.

- How many **potential buyers were shortlisted** in these previous transactions? The idea of this question is to get an understanding of their approach to competitive tension.

- What were the **hardest parts** of the transactions? You are probing to confirm they have real experience, as well as how well they are can guide you around potential problems.

- What is their suggested **sale process** for your business?

- What potential 'strategic value' do they see in your business? Once again, you want them to have given your business some consideration prior to the meeting, and how it fits into the wider industry in which you operate.

- How is **their remuneration structured**, i.e. upfront versus commission, at-risk versus risk-free? Many advisers will charge some level of 'retainer' during the sale process that is not dependent on the sale outcome.

- Who are their **main competitors**, and what sets them apart from their competitors? You will get a better idea of how they deliver their service, and you will also get names of other potential advisers to interview! If they cannot name a competitor, this is a very bad sign.

Not all brokers will add value to the sale process. Many are just glorified real estate agents,[30] with little industry experience and a flawed sales process. You need to identify the duds early and move on.

The broker's mandate

A broker will require you to sign up to a 'mandate'. This is a legally binding document that officially appoints them to represent you. The mandate will oblige you to pay a retainer and commission on a successful sale. It is important that you have this document reviewed by your lawyer, as many of these contain nasty surprises.

When to grant exclusivity to a broker

A broker will usually ask for exclusivity. This is fine, so long as they agree to deliver against certain milestones and allow you to terminate for lack of activity or outcomes against those milestones.

You should also keep any exclusively period as short as possible. How short? This will tie in with the broker's sale process, (which they must be able to outline to you in detail before you sign up). Basically, the broker's exclusivity should end shortly after the time when the buyer is meant to sign the sale agreement.

As a rule, exclusively of around 3 to 6 months should be sufficient. This may be longer if the adviser is going to get involved in preparing your business for sale prior to embarking on the actual sale process.

If a broker offers to 'bring you a buyer' then exclusivity should be limited to that buyer. In fact, this is a way to manage exclusivity by only offering it to a broker to the extent of their intended 'prospect list'. Most brokers will push back hard against this. A broker who is assisting you with a marketing campaign will be able to justify a blanket exclusivity. However, a more targeted broker should accept limited exclusivity.

In a similar way, you can also break exclusivity among locations, or within industries, which match the broker's experience. For example, you would not grant a local broker in Adelaide nationwide exclusivity, unless they can convince you that they also have a contact base in the eastern states.

When to pay a commission

Most brokers will charge a 'success fee' or commission based on the sale value achieved. This can vary from 1% to 3%, depending on the size and complexity of the business and the credibility of the broker. That said, some brokers will try for something higher, like 5-6%. A higher commission, or a minimum 'floor' on the commission may be acceptable for the sale of a small business. This is because the work involved in selling a micro or small business is similar to selling a much larger business.

The commission should be based on the value achieved. Most brokers will expect this to include the value of stock-in-trade or work-in-progress. The key thing to clearly understand is what is and what is not included in the calculation, to ensure the broker's incentives and your own objectives are aligned.

If the sale price is to be paid in instalments, then the payment of commission should match this payment profile. Most brokers will try and have their full commission paid on settlement. Resist this, so the broker does not just roll over when asked for payment terms by buyers.

If the sale price is dependent to some extent on the future performance of the business – or if there is a 'claw-back' mechanism to reduce any deferred payments - then once again the broker's commission needs to match this.

Terminating a mandate

Terminating a broker's mandate may not necessarily end their right to a commission. Most standard broker contracts will provide that the broker still gets a commission if you sell the business within a period of time after their retainer has ended, or if you sell the business to someone they have introduced to you.

Be very careful here. To start with, most brokers do not 'introduce' ready buyers to you. In over 25 years of practicing in this area, we are yet to see a broker introduce a 'ready buyer' (and those that do generally already have a mandate from the buyer). Most brokers will ask you who is likely to be interested in your business, or what categories of people may be interested (e.g. competitors, key suppliers, key customers), and then simply approach them on your behalf. In fact, you may already have spoken to one or more potential buyers prior to engaging a broker.

On the other hand, a broker is going to be legitimately concerned that you will engage them to sell your business, and then after finding you a buyer, terminate their mandate and conclude a deal, thereby avoiding payment of their commission. Practically this would be difficult to do, unless the buyer was only introduced towards the end of the broker's mandate period. Nevertheless, this is a genuine concern.

To balance these competing considerations, we recommend that a commission remain payable for a period of say 6 months from the end of the mandate, and only with respect to buyers who have been introduced or managed by the broker, to the exclusion of anyone you had a relationship with prior to engaging the broker.

Doing it yourself

Depending on how much time and interest you have, you may also wish to consider the alternative of managing the sale process yourself, with the assistance of your existing advisers.

Whether you can do this will depend on your own commercial experience, and the relevant experience of your existing advisers, (i.e. your lawyer, accountant and financier). One purpose of this book is to arm you with the knowledge to make this key choice.

From our observations, people seldom save money representing themselves in a sale process.

14

How we Can Help You

*Find out more about how we can help by visiting our website: **andreyev.com.au**.*

*Call us directly on **1300 654 590** for a chat about your exit strategy.*

Getting 'sale ready'

Andreyev Lawyers can help you prepare your business for sale. Getting a business 'sale ready' involves considering many commercial, contractual and legal issues, all of which we have significant practical experience with.

Increasing your business' value

We can guide and facilitate your business development activities, helping you identify complimentary businesses and opportunities, that when put together with your existing business, may result in a higher overall exit value.

Getting the deal done

Practically, we help our clients plan and execute successful business sales and acquisitions.

We will assist you as a seller with every aspect of the sale process. Likewise, we can assist you as a buyer with every aspect of the purchase process. This includes collating data and preparing your Information Memorandum, providing guidance and advice on the warranty, indemnity, disclosure and due diligence aspects of a sale or purchase, through to documentation and settlement.

Training and mentoring

We can help advisers with little or no practical experience in business sales and acquisitions become comfortable with the legal, regulatory, contractual and commercial issues typically encountered by clients. We do this through training and coaching of both junior staff and seasoned practitioners who are expanding into this area.

About the Author

Andrew Andreyev is the founding Principal of Andreyev Lawyers (andreyev.com.au).

Andrew really enjoys being involved in businesses. He has run his own legal practice since 2001 and holds significant long-term stakes in a software business and real estate agency.

Andrew knows what it feels like to commit funds to an uncertain venture, to bring in partners, and to raise capital from family, friends, and the public. He has also experienced the not-so-pleasant activities of terminating someone's employment, breaking up with a business partner, disagreeing with a supplier, and suing someone to collect a debt.

Andrew regularly advises both the buyers and sellers of businesses across a broad range of transaction values. He has particular expertise in transactions with a cross-border element, or involving a professional investor partner (e.g. private equity and venture capital), where an understanding of pre-deal structuring and taxation considerations is key.

Andrew holds Bachelor degrees in Commerce and Law from Adelaide University, as well as a Master of Laws (in Taxation and International Law) from Melbourne University. He is admitted to practice law in Australia and the United Kingdom, and is a Notary Public in the Supreme Court of South Australia.

Andrew is a Chartered Tax Adviser with the Taxation Institute of Australia (TIA), a Fellow (and a founding member of the Adelaide Chapter) of the Society of Trust & Estate Practitioners (STEP) and a member of the Law Societies of NSW and SA.

Andrew regularly writes and presents on issues facing entrepreneurs, their businesses and their families.

Sources

1   Author of the E-Myth https://www.emyth.com/.

2   Although you may need to put in place an equity plan to attract, retain and incentivise the right people.

3   Published around 2014.

4   2016 Census data and ASBFEO calculations.

5   A balancing charge is the difference between the written-down value of the asset for tax purposes, and the amount you are considered to have received for the asset in the sale. If this is positive, then the balancing charge is assessable to tax. If this is negative, then you may qualify for a tax deduction.

6   See Subdivision 115 *Income Tax Assessment Act 1997* (Cth).

7   See Subdivision 152 *Income Tax Assessment Act 1997* (Cth).

8   Unfortunately, you must accept that whatever information you put into your **Teaser Document** and **Information Memorandum** will ultimately get into the public domain and be available to your competitors. This is inevitable, even if the people you directly provide these documents to sign a well draft **Non-Disclosure Agreements**.

9   For example, under the *Land and Business (Sale and Conveyancing) Act 1994* (SA), and section 52 of the *Estate Agents Act 1980* (Victoria).

10   Including under the *Foreign Acquisitions and Takeovers Act 1975* (Cth) and the *Register of Foreign Ownership of Water or Agricultural Land Act 2015* (Cth).

11   See the 2016 book *Never Split the Difference: Negotiating as if your life depended on it*, by Chris Voss, published by Harper Business.

12   Including the *Privacy Act 1988* (Cth).

13   The agreed 'enterprise value' is typically calculated based on the historical financial accounts, adjusted to reflect a 'cash free, debt free and a normal level of working capital' position.

14   Those tasked with financial due diligence for the buyer should be instructed to analyse the basis on which target entity's historical accounts have been prepared, the basis on which they should have been prepared, and the basis on which the parties agree the completion accounts should

be prepared, and highlight any key discrepancies to the deal team. Otherwise, there is a risk that like will not be compared with like.

15 These conditions often relate to registration of assignments, discharge of liabilities, transfer of telephone numbers and domain registrations, attending to bank account formalities including authorised signatories and other administrative and procedural matters.

16 Of course, many contracts will have 'change of control' provisions that may require you to seek counterparty consent even if you acquire the entity holding the contract.

17 Including deductions for funding and carry-forward of losses.

18 The equity transaction is an input taxed financial supply.

19 For a detailed discussion of the matters that need to be met to qualify as a going concern, see the Tax Office's ruling GSTR 2002/5.

20 Even determining where the business is 'carried on' can be difficult!

21 It is critical that the definition of 'tax liability' in the tax indemnity covers all possible taxes, including income tax, GST, superannuation guarantee amounts, payroll taxes, compensation levies and stamp duty, to name but a few.

22 Both from the perspective of the parties involved and in the broader public interest sense.

23 Return on Equity, or ROE, is simply the percentage of last years' earning against the book value of shareholders' equity.

24 Being 4-6% above the risk-free rate. See *RBA Report: Australian Equity Market Facts 1917-2019*.

25 Each year, the Reserve Bank convenes its Small Business Finance Advisory Panel to better understand the challenges faced by small businesses. The message from the Panel and its surveys continues to be that many small businesses find it challenging to access finance.

26 See RBA Report: https://www.rba.gov.au/publications/bulletin/2018/sep/access-to-small-business-finance.html.

27 See Part 2J.3 of the *Corporations Act 2001* (Cth).

28 See section 260D of the *Corporations Act 2001* (Cth).

29 See section 260B of the *Corporations Act 2001* (Cth).

30 No offence is directed towards real estate agents, but selling a business is a completely different proposition to selling a house.

www.ingramcontent.com/pod-product-compliance
Lightning Source LLC
Chambersburg PA
CBHW041303210326
41598CB00005B/15